D1391597

pasta

Ursula Ferrigno

photography by Peter Cassidy

Quadrille
PUBLISHING

First published in 2009 by
Quadrille Publishing Limited
Alhambra House
27-31 Charing Cross Road
London WC2H OLS

Editorial Director Jane O'Shea
Creative Director Helen Lewis
Editorial Assistant Sarah Jones
Designer Katherine Case
Production Vincent Smith, Ruth Deary

ISBN 978 184400 778 3
Printed in China

Most of the material in this book was previously published as **Truly Madly Pasta**.

Cookery notes
All recipes serve 4 unless otherwise stated. All spoon measures are level
unless otherwise indicated. Follow either metric or imperial measures, not a
mixture of both as they are not necessarily interchangeable. Use fresh herbs
and freshly ground black pepper unless otherwise suggested.

Contents

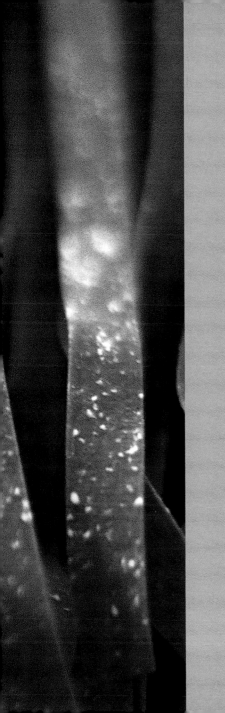

CHAPTER

pasta basics

In Italy, hardly a meal is served without pasta
and it has also become incredibly popular all
over the world. It is, after all, inexpensive,
quick to cook, highly nutritious and extremely
versatile. The range of dried and fresh pastas
available from supermarkets and delicatessens
today is seemingly endless and you can combine
these with all manner of really tasty sauces.

Pasta is an ancient food. Cave drawings
in Imperia, northern Italy, suggest that it was
there long before Marco Polo reportedly brought
it back from China. Pasta is fundamental to
Italian life. It is a daily ritual, consumed at
every lunch or dinner, even on Christmas Day,
as part of the first course, **primo piatto**, after
the **antipasti** and before the main course, and
it is never a whole meal on its own.

Pasta was once a southern speciality,
while in the north they favoured rice and
polenta, but pasta has somehow united Italy
and it is now eaten the length and breadth of
the country. Pasta is the soul of Italian life.

During the Renaissance, pasta – especially lasagne, ravioli and tortellini – was found only on the tables of the wealthy. In the nineteenth century, though, it came to be viewed as food for the poor, especially in Naples. In the twentieth century, Mussolini went so far as to consider banning it from the Italian army's diet because he thought it made the soldiers lethargic!

From a nutritional angle, pasta is a complex carbohydrate food, but, because it has a low fat content, it isn't high in calories at all (of course, some of the sauces served with it can be). Some varieties of pasta, notably those made with eggs, contain as much as 13 per cent protein, as well as useful vitamins and minerals.

One's imagination can run riot with ingredients to include in a pasta sauce: you can use vegetables, pulses, cheeses, oils, herbs and spices. I eat pasta every day; it's the only thing that I know I will definitely do each day. My grandfather used to say, 'I'm not living if I haven't eaten pasta every day'.

Types of pasta

Fresh egg pasta (**pasta fresca all'uovo**) bought vacuum-sealed can be limp and tasteless, but Italian food shops that make pasta on the premises sell something nearer the real thing. Dried pasta (**pasta secca**) is good, especially if made in Italy from durum semolina (**pasta di semola di grano duro secca**), and there are types of dried egg pasta (**pasta all'uovo secca**). However, the ultimate pasta is homemade. Most of the recipes that I have included in this book use the simple pastas, such as spaghetti, tagliatelle and lasagne — those which are most often used at home, **a casa**, in Italy. This saves having many half-used packages of different shapes cluttering your cupboards.

Making pasta

Pasta should be made from strong flour rich in the gluten that gives pasta its true texture. The wheat is very finely milled to produce '00' grade flour, which is soft and silky. It is available from good delicatessens and Italian delis. Plain flour may be used, but the pasta will be softer.

Basic egg pasta

MAKES ABOUT 1KG/2¼LB

350g/12oz plain flour, preferably Italian 00
350g/12oz semolina flour
1tsp sea salt

7 medium eggs (preferably corn-fed and Italian, so the yolks are yellow)
2 tbsp olive oil

1 Pile the flours on a work surface, then blend them together, adding the salt, into one large volcano-like pile with a crater-like reservoir in the centre.

2 Break the eggs into the reservoir and add the oil. With a fork, slowly break up the eggs and draw in the flour with the other hand to make a paste. When all the flour is mixed in you should have a ball of dough – if it seems too dry, add a little more oil or water, if it seems too damp knead in a little more flour.

3 At first the mixture will be soft and claggy, but knead until it is smooth and silken, and when you press a finger into it the depression bounces back. Wrap in cling film and allow to rest in the refrigerator for about 30 minutes.

This will make enough dough to serve 12. It is easier to deal with larger quantities. You can keep the dough in the fridge for several days or freeze what you don't need immediately.

Pile the flours onto a work surface and blend together, adding the salt, into a volcano-like pile.

Break the eggs in the crater-like reservoir and add the oil. Using a fork, slowly break up the eggs.

Draw in the flour with your other hand to create a paste.

When all the flour is thoroughly mixed in you should be left with a ball of dough.

If the mixture seems to dry then add a little more oil or water, if it seems too damp knead in a little more flour.

At first the mixture will seem soft and claggy, but keep kneading, collecting up the loose bits of dough.

Knead until the dough is smooth and silken and when you press a finger into it the depression bounces back.

Wrap the ball of dough in clingfilm and allow to rest in the refrigerator for about 30 minutes.

Using a pasta machine

Roll out the rested chilled pasta dough to a long thinnish oval that will just fit into the width of the pasta machine. Starting with the machine rollers set at their widest possible setting, pass the dough through the machine several times.

Change the machine rollers to the next widest setting and repeat the process. Continue down the settings in this way. By the time you have passed the dough several times through the setting one up from the narrowest (I never use the narrowest setting as I find it produces pasta that is so fine that it is too difficult to handle), the pasta should be ready for shaping. It should be thin enough for you to be able to make out your fingers through the sheet as shown overleaf.

For things like ravioli and lasagne you can use these pasta sheets just as they are, trimming them to the required shape. To make pasta noodles, however, pass the dough through the selected cutters to produce the shape required. Leave to dry in lengths for 5—7 minutes (otherwise the pasta will stick to itself), then wind handfuls of the lengths of pasta into nests, as shown, and leave them to dry again briefly before cooking.

Roll out the rested chilled pasta to a long thinnish oval that will just fit into the width of the pasta machine.

With the machine rollers set at their widest setting, pass the dough through the machine several times.

Change the machine rollers to the next widest setting and repeat the process.

Continue down the settings in this way until you are one up from the narrowest setting. Pass it through several times.

The pasta is now ready for shaping. It should be thin enough to be able to make out your fingers through the sheet.

To make pasta noodles, pass the dough through the selected cutters to produce the required shape.

Leave the pasta to dry in lengths for about 5–7 minutes, otherwise it will stick to itself.

Wind handfuls of the pasta into nests and leave to dry again briefly before cooking.

For pasta nero (squid ink pasta): simply add a
4g sachet of squid ink with the eggs and oil.
Sachets of squid ink can be found in good
fishmongers and Italian delis.

For paste verde or pasta con spinaci: replace 2 of the eggs with 500g/1lb 2oz spinach cooked in a tightly closed pan (in the water clinging to it after washing) for a few minutes until tender and then allowed to cool. You need to remove as much moisture from it as possible.

Matching sauces to pasta shapes

Pasta is made in hundreds of different shapes, each with a different ability to cling to the all-important sauce. A simple rule-of-thumb is that hollow or twisted shapes take chunky sauces and that the flatter the pasta, the richer the sauce. Thin and long pasta suits an oily, more liquid sauce; more complicated shapes will have holes and curves in which a thicker sauce can nestle and cling.

Heavy sauces with large chunks of meat are unlikely to go well with thin spaghettini or tagliolini, simply because the chunks will slide off, so these sauces are always served with a wide pasta such as pappardelle, maccheroni and tagliatelle or with short tubular shapes such as penne, fusilli, conchiglie and rigatoni.

In the south of Italy, olive oil is used for cooking rather than butter, so there sauces tend to be made with olive oil and they are usually served with dried plain durum wheat pasta (**pasta di semola grano duro**), such as spaghetti and vermicelli. These long thin shapes are traditionally served with tomato and seafood sauces, most of which are made with olive oil, and with light vegetable sauces. Spaghetti and vermicelli are also ideal vehicles for minimalist sauces. Grated cheese is not normally used in these sauces, nor is it sprinkled over them.

In the north, butter and cream are used in sauces and, unsurprisingly, these go well with the egg pasta that is made there, which absorbs butter and cream and makes the sauce cling to it. Butter and cream also go well with tomato sauces when these are served with short shapes especially penne, rigatoni, farfalle and fusilli.

Amounts of pasta to cook per person:
Dried pasta 75–115g/3–4oz
Fresh pasta 115–150g/4–5oz
Filled pasta 175–200g/6–7oz

Cooking pasta

Cook pasta in rapidly boiling water, bring back to the boil as quickly as possible and keep at a rolling boil until done. Always cook dried pasta in a large pan so that there is plenty of room for the pasta to expand, as it absorbs the water. Only add salt when the water is boiling; if it is put in too early it will disperse around the sides of the pan and the water will not be salty enough.

DRIED PASTA, which is made from durum wheat, is ready when it is **al dente** (literally 'to the tooth'), that is tender but with a central resistance to the bite. You will see that I have repeated this in full in every recipe and for this I make no apology.

FRESH PASTA made from a softer wheat, is never as firm as dried when cooked, but it should have some resistance. Overcooked pasta of any kind is limp and unpalatable. An Italian cook would never serve it.

STUFFED PASTA SHAPES require gentle handling or they may burst open and release their filling into the water. Add them to boiling water, bring back to the boil quickly, then reduce the heat and poach the pasta shapes at a gentle simmer, stirring them gently during cooking.

SPAGHETTI and other LONG DRIED PASTA will need to be coiled into the boiling water as it softens. Take a handful at a time and dip it in the boiling water so that it touches the bottom of the pan. As the spaghetti strands soften, coil them round using a wooden spoon or fork until they are all submerged.

FRESH PASTA generally takes far less time to cook; it can be as rapid as 4–5 minutes, although this depends on the shape and size. Homemade tagliatelle can actually cook in as little as 30 seconds.

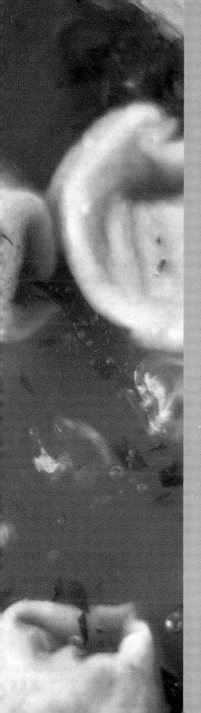

pasta
soups &
stocks

Pasta in soup is very much a part of traditional Italian home cooking, although its role in this respect is rather overlooked abroad. Served as a **primo piatto** instead of an ordinary pasta dish, it is seen as highly digestible energy-giving food for fuel. Usually made with lots of added vegetables and/or pulses, it makes the ultimate comfort food in winter. Importantly, the Italians don't regard soups as a repository for leftovers, but use the best and freshest of ingredients and put some energy into making the tastiest of stocks on which to base their pasta **in brodo**.

Minestrone with pasta & roasted vegetables

SERVES 4-6

200g/7oz fresh ripe tomatoes
3 tbsp olive oil
1 onion
2 celery stalks
2 medium carrots
1 courgette, thinly sliced
1 potato cut into 1cm/½in cubes
150g/5oz French beans, in 5cm/2in pieces

¼ Savoy cabbage shredded
3 garlic cloves, finely chopped
3 fresh bay leaves
200g/7oz cooked cannellini beans
1.2 litres/2 pints vegetable stock
sea salt and freshly ground black pepper
90g/3¼oz dried vermicelli or maltagliati
   freshly grated Parmesan cheese, to serve

1 Preheat the oven to 200°C/400°F/Gas 6. Remove their stems and place the tomatoes in a roasting tin. Drizzle with a little of the olive oil and roast in the oven for 20–30 minutes, depending on their size, until they begin to colour and the skins split. Remove from the oven and cool slightly before peeling off the skins. Chop roughly.

2 Chop the onion, celery and carrots into dice. Drizzle over a little olive oil and mix to coat the vegetables lightly. Season, spread in a single layer on an oven tray and roast for 5–10 minutes. Add the courgette and potato and return to the oven for another 5–10 minutes, until the onions and carrots are starting to caramelize and the courgettes and potatoes are lightly browned.

3 Heat the last of the oil in a large saucepan and stir-fry the French beans, cabbage and garlic for 3 minutes. Add the bay leaves, cannellini beans and all the roasted vegetables. Pour in the stock with salt and pepper to taste. Bring to the boil, stir well, cover and simmer for 30 minutes, until the vegetables are tender, stirring occasionally.

4 Break the pasta into small pieces and add to the soup. Simmer, stirring often, for 6–8 minutes, until the pasta is al dente, i.e. just tender but still firm to the bite. Adjust the seasoning if necessary. Serve in warm bowls, sprinkled with Parmesan.

Genoese minestrone with pesto

SERVES 4-6

1 onion
2 celery stalks
2 medium carrots
3 tbsp olive oil
150g/5oz French beans, cut into
    5cm/2in pieces
1 courgette, thinly sliced
1 potato, cut into 1cm/½in cubes
¼ Savoy cabbage, shredded
200g/7oz cooked or rinsed canned
    cannellini beans

2 Italian plum tomatoes, chopped
1.2 litres/2 pints vegetable stock
sea salt and freshly ground black pepper
90g/3¼oz dried vermicelli or maltagliati

FOR THE PESTO

1 garlic clove
2 tsp pine nuts
2 tbsp extra-virgin olive oil
1 tbsp freshly grated Parmesan cheese
1 tbsp freshly grated Pecorino cheese
20 basil leaves

1 Chop the onion, celery and carrot finely. Heat the oil in a large saucepan, add the chopped vegetables and cook over a low heat, stirring frequently for 5–7 minutes.

2 Mix in the French beans, courgette, potato and cabbage. Stir-fry over a medium heat for 3 minutes. Add the cannellini beans and tomatoes. Stir-fry for 2–3 minutes.

3 Add the stock with salt and pepper to taste. Bring to the boil, stir well, cover and simmer, stirring occasionally, until all the vegetables are tender – about 40 minutes.

4 Meanwhile, make the pesto using a pestle and mortar: pound the garlic with the pine nuts, then add the oil, cheeses and basil in that order until you have a thick sauce. You can use a food processor, but then the flavour will not be as pungent.

5 Break the pasta into small pieces and add to the soup. Simmer, stirring often, for 5 minutes. Add the pesto sauce and stir it in well, then simmer for 2–3 minutes more or until the pasta is al dente, i.e. tender but still firm to the bite.

6 Taste and adjust the seasoning if necessary. Serve in warmed bowls.

Minestrone with pasta & chickpeas

SERVES 4–6

4 tbsp olive oil
1 onion, finely chopped
2 carrots, finely chopped
2 celery stalks, finely chopped
400g/14oz cooked chickpeas
200g/7oz cooked or rinsed canned
  cannellini beans
150ml/¼ pint passata
2 fresh rosemary sprigs
sea salt and freshly ground black pepper
200g/7oz conchiglie (pasta shells)
freshly grated Parmesan cheese, to serve

FOR THE VEGETABLE STOCK

1 onion, halved
7 cloves
3 celery stalks
2 carrots
2–3 leeks
handful of potato peelings, well cleaned
2 garlic cloves, halved
a little olive oil
3 fresh bay leaves, torn
handful of flat-leaf parsley with stalks

1 First make the vegetable stock: stud the onion halves with the cloves and coarsely chop the other vegetables. Heat the oil in a large heavy-based saucepan and gently sauté all these vegetables. Add the remaining ingredients with cold water to cover. Season lightly. Bring to the boil, skim, lower the heat and simmer for 25–35 minutes.

2 Towards the end of this time, heat the oil in a large saucepan, add the finely chopped vegetables and cook over a low heat, stirring frequently, for 5–7 minutes. Add the chickpeas and cannellini beans, stir well, then cook for 5 minutes. Stir in the passata and 125ml/4fl oz water, and cook, stirring, for 2–3 minutes. Add 600ml/1 pint of the sieved stock, 1 rosemary sprig and salt and pepper to taste. Bring to the boil, cover then simmer gently, stirring occasionally, for 1 hour.

3 Add another 1 litre/1¾ pint of sieved stock and the pasta, and bring to the boil, stirring. Lower the heat and simmer, stirring frequently, until the pasta is al dente, i.e. tender but still firm to the bite, 7–8 minutes. Taste and adjust the seasoning.

4 Remove the rosemary sprig and serve the soup hot in warmed bowls, topped with grated Parmesan and fresh rosemary leaves.

Farmhouse soup

SERVES 4–6

2 tbsp olive oil
1 onion, roughly chopped
3 carrots
175–200g/6–7oz turnips
175g/6oz swede
400g/14oz can of chopped tomatoes
1 tbsp tomato purée
handful of mixed fresh herbs, such as
  rosemary, thyme and parsley
1 tsp dried oregano
sea salt and freshly ground black pepper
1.5 litres/2½ pints vegetable stock
  (see page 33) or water
50g/2oz dried small macaroni
400g/14oz cooked or rinsed canned borlotti
  or cannellini beans
handful of parsley, to garnish
freshly grated Parmesan, to serve

1 Heat the oil in a large saucepan, add the onion and cook over a low heat for about 5 minutes until softened.

2 Cut all the fresh vegetables into large chunks and add them with the canned tomatoes, tomato purée, fresh herbs and dried oregano with salt and pepper to taste. Pour in the stock or water and bring to the boil. Stir well, cover, lower the heat and simmer for 30 minutes, stirring occasionally.

3 Add the pasta and bring to the boil, stirring. Lower the heat and simmer, uncovered and stirring frequently, until the pasta is just al dente, i.e. tender but still firm to the bite, about 5 minutes.

4 Stir in the beans and heat through for 2–3 minutes, then remove from the heat and stir in the parsley. Taste the soup and adjust the seasoning.

5 Serve hot in warmed soup bowls, with grated Parmesan handed round separately.

Clam & pasta soup

SERVES 4-6

225g/8oz clams
a little plain flour
2 tbsp olive oil
1 onion, finely chopped
leaves from 1 fresh thyme sprig,
   plus extra for garnish
2 garlic cloves, crushed

5–6 basil leaves, torn, plus extra for garnish
½ tsp chilli flakes
1 litre/1¾ pints fish stock
350ml/12fl oz passata
1 tsp sugar
sea salt and freshly ground black pepper
85g/3oz fresh peas
65g/2¼oz dried small pasta shapes

1 Keep the clams submerged in water with a little added plain flour (this helps plump them up and purge them of dirt). Discard clams that remain open when tapped.

2 Heat the oil in a large saucepan, add the onion and cook gently for 5 minutes, until softened but not coloured. Add the thyme, then stir in the garlic, basil, chilli, stock, passata and sugar, with salt and pepper to taste. Bring to the boil, then lower the heat and simmer gently, stirring occasionally, for 15 minutes. Add the peas and cook for a further 5 minutes.

3 Add the pasta and bring to the boil, stirring. Lower the heat and simmer, stirring frequently, until the pasta is only just al dente, i.e. tender but still firm to the bite, about 5 minutes.

4 Turn the heat down to low, add the clams and cook for 5–7 minutes until the clams open (discard any that stubbornly refuse to). Adjust the seasoning.

5 Serve hot, garnished with extra basil and thyme.

If pressed, you can make a fairly reputable version of this dish with canned clams – but look for an Italian brand and rinse them well!

Any fish can be used in this stew; a white fish like haddock can replace the snapper, and I have made it with plaice and sea bass.

Sardinian fish stew

SERVES 4-6

5 tbsp olive oil

4 garlic cloves, finely chopped

½ small fresh red chilli, deseeded and
finely chopped

1 large handful of flat-leaf parsley,
roughly chopped

1 red snapper, about 450g/1lb, cleaned
and with head and tail removed

1 red or grey mullet, about 500g/1¼lb,
cleaned and with head and tail removed

350g–450g/12oz–1lb thick cod fillet

400g/14oz can of chopped Italian plum
tomatoes

sea salt and freshly ground black pepper

175g/6oz dried fregula, pastina or pantaletti

1 Heat 2 tablespoons of the olive oil in a large flameproof casserole. Add the
chopped garlic and chilli with about half the chopped parsley. Fry over a medium
heat, stirring occasionally, for about 5 minutes, taking care not to brown the garlic.

2 Cut all of the fish into large chunks, leaving the skin and bones in place in the
case of the snapper and mullet, adding the pieces to the casserole as you cut them.
Sprinkle with a further 2 tablespoons of the olive oil and fry for a few minutes more.

3 Add the tomatoes, then fill the empty can with water and pour this into the pan.
Bring to the boil. Stir in a little salt and pepper to taste, lower the heat and cook for
10 minutes, stirring occasionally.

4 Add the fregula or pasta and simmer for 5 minutes. Add 250ml/9fl oz of water
and the remaining oil. Simmer for 15 minutes.

5 If the soup becomes too thick, add more water. Taste and adjust the seasoning.
Serve hot in warm bowls, sprinkled with the remaining parsley.

Fregula is actually a type of cous cous,
but any small soup pasta can be used instead.

Pasta in meat broth

SERVES 4–6

about 450g/1lb meat bones (any type, or a
    mixture, will do — ask your butcher)
3 fresh bay leaves
sea salt and freshly ground black pepper
2 ripe tomatoes

65g/2¼oz small soup pasta, such
    as farfalline (little farfalle)
1 tbsp extra-virgin olive oil
25g/1oz freshly grated Parmesan cheese
handful of flat-leaf parsley, finely chopped

1 Preheat the oven to 200°C/400°F/Gas 6. Put the bones in a large roasting tin and roast in the preheated oven for 25 minutes, until well coloured.

2 Put the browned bones in a large pan and cover with water. Add the bay leaves and season with salt. Bring to the boil and skim well. Simmer gently for 40 minutes, skimming from time-to-time if necessary. Strain.

3 Meanwhile, put the tomatoes in a bowl and cover with boiling water. Leave for about 40 seconds then plunge them into cold water. Using a sharp knife, peel off the skins and finely chop the flesh, discarding the seeds.

4 Add the tomatoes to the strained stock and cook for 2–3 minutes more.

5 Stir in the pasta and cook for 3–5 minutes until it is just tender. Season with salt and pepper to taste and stir in the olive oil.

6 Serve sprinkled with Parmesan cheese and parsley.

Pasta soup with peas & chicken livers

SERVES 4–6

115g/4oz fresh chicken livers
1 tbsp olive oil
knob of unsalted butter
4 garlic cloves, crushed
3 sprigs of parsley
3 sprigs of marjoram
3 sprigs of sage

leaves from a sprig of fresh thyme
sea salt and freshly ground black pepper
1–2 tbsp dry white wine
1.2 litres/2 pints chicken stock
4 medium potatoes, peeled and cubed
225g/8oz fresh peas, shelled
50g/2oz dried pasta shapes, such as farfalle
    handful of basil

1 Trim the chicken livers and cut into small pieces (this is best done with scissors). Chop the herbs.

2 Heat the oil and butter in a frying pan, add the garlic and herbs, with salt and pepper to taste, and fry gently for a few minutes. Add the livers, increase the heat to high and stir-fry for a few minutes until they change colour and become dry. Pour the wine over and cook until it evaporates, then remove from the heat, taste and adjust the seasoning.

3 Put the chicken stock in a large saucepan with some seasoning and bring to the boil. Add the potatoes and the peas, and simmer for 5 minutes, then add the pasta. Bring the soup back to the boil, stirring, and allow to simmer, stirring frequently, until the pasta is just al dente, i.e. tender but still firm to the bite, about 5 minutes.

4 Add the fried chicken livers and basil, and warm through, adjust the seasoning and serve hot in warmed bowls.

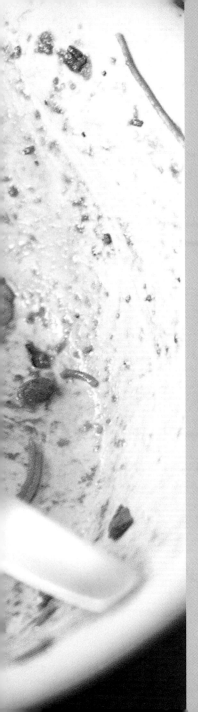

pasta
instant

Pasta is one of the easiest of foods to cook in a hurry. In the 10 minutes or so it takes to cook most dried pastas, there are lots of wonderful tasty sauces that can be made. Some can even be put together in the minutes that fresh pasta needs and a few can literally be made at the table. The secret to enjoying any number of fast pasta dishes is having the right things in your storecupboard, like good oil, canned Italian plum tomatoes, canned cannelini or borlotti beans or chickpeas, and some cans of anchovies, tuna and vongole. With a good chunk of Parmesan in the fridge, together with eggs, cream and possibly some bacon or pancetta, you can conjure up a veritable feast. A couple of fresh herbs, such as parsley, chives or basil, will heighten the magic.

Spaghetti with fresh tomato sauce

SERVES 2
200g/7oz spaghetti
sea salt and freshly ground black pepper
6 ripe tomatoes
2 garlic cloves, crushed

3 tbsp olive oil
50g/2oz freshly grated Parmesan cheese,
  plus extra to serve
handful of torn fresh basil leaves

1 Cook the spaghetti in a large saucepan of boiling salted water until just al dente, i.e. tender but still firm to the bite.

2 Meanwhile, chop the tomatoes and put in a bowl with the garlic, olive oil, Parmesan cheese, basil, salt and pepper. Mix together.

3 Drain the cooked pasta and toss with the sauce. Serve immediately with extra grated cheese if wished.

Pasta with raw tomato sauce

SERVES 4

350g/12oz pasta of your choice
500g/1¼lb ripe Italian plum tomatoes
1 large handful of fresh basil leaves
5 tbsp extra-virgin olive oil

115g/4oz ricotta salata, diced
1 garlic clove, crushed
sea salt and freshly ground black pepper
coarsely shaved Pecorino cheese, to serve

1 Cook the pasta in a pan of salted boiling water until al dente, i.e. just tender but still firm to the bite.

2 Meanwhile, roughly chop the plum tomatoes, removing the cores and as many of the seeds as you can. Tear the basil leaves into shreds with your fingers.

3 Put all the ingredients except the Pecorino in a bowl with salt and pepper to taste and stir well. (If you are not in a hurry, it is a good idea at this point to cover the bowl and leave at room temperature for 1–2 hours, to let the flavours mingle. Obviously you wouldn't cook the pasta until then either.)

4 Taste the sauce and adjust the seasoning if necessary, then toss it with the hot cooked pasta. Serve immediately, with the Pecorino handed round separately.

Ricotta salata is a salted and dried version of ricotta. It is firmer than traditional soft white ricotta, and can easily be crumbled, diced or grated. Young soft Pecorino can be used in its place.

Spaghetti with red pepper & tomatoes

SERVES 4

375g/13oz spaghetti

sea salt and freshly ground black pepper

600g/1lb 5oz ripe tomatoes

½ garlic clove

1 sweet red pepper, deseeded and sliced

handful of fresh mint leaves

3 tbsp fruity extra-virgin olive oil, ideally
finest estate-bottled

handful of fresh basil leaves

50g/2oz freshly grated Parmesan cheese

1 Cook the spaghetti in a large saucepan of boiling salted water until just al dente, i.e. tender but still firm to the bite.

2 Meanwhile, scald the tomatoes with boiling water, then skin them. Cut them in half and remove the seeds.

3 Place the tomatoes in a food processor with salt and pepper to taste, the garlic, sliced red pepper and mint. Blend well until the sauce becomes smooth and uniform. Adjust the seasoning if necessary.

4 Drain the spaghetti well and return to the pan. Add the fruity extra-virgin oil, the puréed sauce and the basil, and mix well. Serve with the cheese.

Alfredo's fettuccine with cream & cheese

SERVES 4

50g/2oz unsalted butter

200ml/7fl oz double cream

50g/2oz freshly grated Parmesan cheese,
plus extra to serve

sea salt and freshly ground black pepper

350g/12oz fresh fettuccine or tagliatelle

1 Melt the butter in a large saucepan, add the cream and bring to just below boiling point. Simmer for 5 minutes, stirring, then add the Parmesan, with salt and pepper to taste, and turn off the heat under the pan.

2 Bring a large saucepan of salted water to the boil. Drop in all the pasta and quickly bring back to the boil, stirring occasionally. Cook until al dente, 2–3 minutes. Drain well.

3 Turn the heat under the pan of cream to low, add the pasta and toss until it is coated in the sauce. Taste for seasoning. Serve at once with extra cheese if necessary.

Penne with broad beans & ricotta

SERVES 4

150g/5oz shelled broad beans
200g/7oz penne
sea salt and freshly ground black pepper
1 tbsp olive oil

1 garlic clove, crushed
25g/1oz freshly grated Pecorino cheese
50g/2oz ricotta
about 2 tbsp extra-virgin olive oil
fresh marjoram leaves, to garnish

1 Steam the broad beans for 6 minutes until tender.

2 Meanwhile, cook the penne in a large saucepan of boiling salted water for about 10 minutes until just al dente, i.e. tender but still firm to the bite.

3 Heat the olive oil in a saucepan and fry the garlic until lightly browned.

4 Drain the pasta and add to the pan with the broad beans, ricotta and Pecorino, extra-virgin olive oil, and some salt and pepper. Toss well together.

5 Serve garnished with marjoram leaves.

Bucatini with courgettes

SERVES 4
375g/13oz bucatini
sea salt and freshly ground black pepper
150ml/¼ pint olive oil
450g/1lb small tender courgettes
115g/4oz Parmesan cheese, freshly grated,
  plus more to serve if you like
115g/4oz sweet Provolone cheese, freshly
  grated, plus more to serve if you like
50g/2oz unsalted butter, cut into pieces
handful of basil leaves, torn
handful of mint leaves, torn
1 garlic clove, crushed
2 tbsp fruity extra-virgin olive oil

1 Cook the bucatini in a large saucepan of boiling salted water until just al dente, i.e. tender but still firm to the bite.

2 Meanwhile, heat the olive oil in a sauté pan. Cut the courgettes into thin slices and fry these, a few at a time, in the hot oil until lightly golden. Remove and place in a large bowl.

3 Add the two cheeses, butter, basil, mint and garlic to the bowl, and season with salt and pepper.

4 Drain the cooked pasta thoroughly and mix well with the contents of the bowl.

5 Serve immediately, drizzled with the fruity extra virgin olive oil and with extra cheese if desired.

Bucatini are the long hollow noodles, like slightly fatter spaghetti but with a hole down the middle to help them cook faster.

Fettuccine with chickpeas

SERVES 4

350g/12oz fettuccine
sea salt and freshly ground black pepper
6 flavoursome tomatoes or
   200g/7oz vine-ripened cherry tomatoes
4 tbsp olive oil
2 garlic cloves, crushed
generous handful chopped flat-leaf parsley

400g/14oz can of chickpeas, drained
  and rinsed
2 tbsp fruity fine extra-virgin olive oil
generous quantity of freshly grated
  Parmesan cheese, to serve
generous handful of freshly torn basil
  leaves, to serve

1 Cook the pasta in a large pan of boiling salted water until just al dente, i.e. tender but still firm to the bite.

2 Meanwhile, put the tomatoes in a bowl and cover with boiling water. Leave for about 40 seconds then plunge them into cold water. Using a sharp knife, peel off the skins and chop the flesh. If using vine-ripened tomatoes, just halve.

3 Heat the olive oil in a medium-sized saucepan and gently cook the garlic. Add the tomatoes, parsley and chickpeas, salt and pepper. Cover and set aside.

4 Drain the pasta when ready and toss in the fruity fine extra-virgin olive oil and the chickpea mixture. Adjust the seasoning to taste.

5 Serve in warmed bowls with lashings of cheese and basil leaves.

For a version with fewer fat calories, replace the cream with bread soaked in milk and whiz this with the nuts in the food processor.

Pasta shells with walnuts & mushrooms

SERVES 4

115g/4oz dried wild mushrooms,
  preferably porcini
350g/12oz conchiglie (pasta shells)
sea salt and freshly ground black pepper
85g/3oz walnuts
handful of basil leaves
handful of young sage leaves
200ml/7fl oz single cream
1 large garlic clove
25g/1oz unsalted butter
50g/2oz freshly grated Parmesan cheese

1 Soak the dried mushrooms in warm water to cover for 10 minutes.

2 Meanwhile, cook the pasta in a large saucepan of boiling salted water until al dente, i.e. tender but still firm to the bite.

3 While the pasta cooks, finely chop the walnuts, tear the basil and chop the sage. Add the cream, season with salt and pepper, and mix together.

4 Crush the garlic. Drain the mushrooms and pat dry. Chop any that are too large. Melt the butter in a frying pan, add the garlic and fry it gently for 2–3 minutes. Stir in the mushrooms and cream sauce. Warm through gently.

5 Drain the cooked pasta and add to the mixture, stirring well. Serve sprinkled with Parmesan cheese.

Farfalle with Gorgonzola cream

SERVES 4

350g/12oz dried farfalle

sea salt and freshly ground black pepper

175g/6oz Gorgonzola cheese (at room temperature), rind removed and cut into very small dice

150ml/¼ pint double cream

pinch of sugar

2 tsp finely chopped fresh sage, plus fresh sage leaves, shredded, to garnish

1 Cook the pasta in a large pan of boiling salted water for about 10 minutes until just al dente, i.e. tender but still firm to the bite.

2 Drain the cooked pasta and return it to the pan in which it was cooked. Add the Gorgonzola, cream, sugar, plenty of black pepper and the chopped sage. Toss over a medium heat until the pasta is evenly coated. Taste and adjust the seasoning with more salt if necessary.

3 Divide between 4 warmed bowls. Garnish each portion with fresh sage leaves and serve immediately.

This northern dish makes the most of tasty Gorgonzola. You could try the dolce variety if you prefer a milder cheese flavour.

Rigatoni with pine nuts & Gorgonzola

SERVES 2

65g/2¼oz broccoli florets
65g/2¼oz cauliflower florets
200g/7oz rigatoni
sea salt and freshly ground black pepper

45g/1½oz pine nuts
2 tbsp olive oil
1 red onion, finely chopped
1 tsp chopped fresh thyme
115g/4oz Gorgonzola cheese

1 Steam the broccoli and cauliflower florets for about 12 minutes, depending on their size, until tender.

2 At the same time, cook the rigatoni in a large saucepan of boiling salted water until just al dente, i.e. tender but still firm to the bite.

3 Meanwhile, spread the pine nuts onto a sheet of foil and toast under the grill, turning them frequently.

4 Heat the oil in a saucepan and fry the onion until it has softened. Add the thyme, salt and pepper.

5 Cut the cheese into cubes and add to the onion, along with the toasted nuts, broccoli and cauliflower.

6 Drain the pasta and toss into the mixture. Adjust the seasoning to taste and serve.

Rigatoni are large pasta tubes which are ribbed on the outside. Their size and shape suit strongly flavoured sauces well. Fusilli is equally good in this recipe.

Spaghetti with tomatoes & pancetta

SERVES 4

350g/12oz ripe plum tomatoes
150g/5oz pancetta, diced
2 tbsp olive oil
1 onion, finely chopped
sea salt and freshly ground black pepper

350g/12oz fresh or dried spaghetti
handful of fresh marjoram sprigs, with their
    leaves stripped
generous amount of freshly grated Pecorino
    cheese, to serve

1 Chop the ripe plum tomatoes into chunky dice.

2 Put the pancetta in a medium saucepan with the oil. Stir over a low heat until the fat runs. Add the onion and stir to mix. Cook gently for about 5 minutes, stirring.

3 Add the tomatoes with salt and pepper to taste. Stir well and cook for 7 minutes.

4 Meanwhile, cook the pasta a large pan of boiling salted water until just al dente, i.e. tender but still firm to the bite.

5 Remove the sauce from the heat and stir in the marjoram. Taste and adjust the seasoning if necessary.

6 Drain the pasta and tip into a warmed serving bowl. Pour the sauce over the pasta and toss well. Serve immediately in warmed bowls. Hand round the grated Pecorino separately for people to add.

You can buy packets of ready-diced pancetta in most supermarkets. Bacon can be substituted but the sauce will not taste the same.

This is really just a smartened-up version of Spaghetti alla Carbonara, named after Roman charcoal workers said to have devised it.

Vermicelli with saffron

SERVES 4

350g/12oz dried vermicelli
sea salt and freshly ground black pepper
large pinch of saffron strands
150g/5oz cooked ham, cut into strips

200ml/7fl oz double cream
50g/2oz freshly grated Parmesan cheese,
 plus extra to serve
2 egg yolks

1 Cook the vermicelli in a large saucepan of boiling salted water until just al dente, i.e. tender but still firm to the bite.

2 While the pasta cooks, put the saffron strands in a saucepan, add 2 tablespoons of water and bring to the boil immediately. Remove the pan from the heat and leave it to sit for a while.

3 Add the ham to the saucepan containing the saffron, and stir in the cream and Parmesan with a little salt and pepper to taste. Heat gently, stirring all the time. When the cream starts to bubble, remove the sauce from the heat and add the egg yolks, beating well to mix. Taste and adjust the seasoning.

4 Add the drained vermicelli, mix well and serve in warmed bowls, with a little extra cheese if you wish.

Spaghetti with tuna, pancetta & mushrooms

SERVES 4

25g/1oz dried porcini mushrooms
175ml/6fl oz warm water
2 tbsp olive oil
1 garlic clove
85g/3oz pancetta or rindless streaky bacon,
  cut into 5mm/¼in slices

225g/8oz button mushrooms, chopped
sea salt and freshly ground black pepper
350g/12oz dried spaghetti
200g/7oz can of tuna (preferably in olive oil),
  drained

1 Put the porcini in a small bowl, pour over the warm water and leave them to soak for 15 minutes.

2 Meanwhile, heat the oil in a large saucepan, add the garlic clove and cook gently for about 2 minutes, crushing it with a wooden spoon to release the flavour. Remove the garlic and discard. Add the pancetta or bacon to the oil remaining in the pan and cook for 3–4 minutes, stirring occasionally.

3 Drain the porcini, reserving the soaking liquid, and chop them finely.

4 Add both types of mushroom to the saucepan and cook, stirring, for 1–2 minutes, then add 6 tablespoons of the reserved mushroom soaking liquid. Season with salt and pepper to taste. Simmer for 5 minutes.

5 Meanwhile, cook the pasta in boiling salted water until al dente, i.e. just tender but still firm to the bite, adding the remaining mushroom soaking liquid to the pasta cooking water.

6 Flake the drained canned tuna into the mushroom sauce and fold it in gently. Taste and adjust the seasoning.

7 Drain the cooked pasta well and tip it into a warmed serving bowl. Pour the sauce over the top, toss well and serve immediately.

You could replace the canned tuna with canned sardines – or maybe use some grilled fresh tuna.

The best flavour comes from vacuum-packed slices of mullet bottarga, which are easy to grate. Keep leftovers wrapped in the fridge.

Macaroni with dried tuna roe

SERVES 4
350g/12oz maccheroni
sea salt and freshly ground black pepper
2 tbsp olive oil
1 garlic clove, sliced
10 cherry tomatoes, halved
½ glass of dry white wine

handful of flat-leaf parsley chopped
2 tbsp extra-virgin olive oil
85g/3oz bottarga di tonno, diced very small

FOR THE CREMA
2 garlic cloves
25g/1oz pine nuts, preferably Italian

1 Cook the maccheroni in a large saucepan of boiling salted water for 10 minutes until just al dente, i.e. tender but still firm to the bite.

2 Meanwhile, make the crema: using a pestle and mortar, crush the garlic cloves and the pine nuts to a cream.

3 In a medium-sized saucepan, heat the olive oil and add the sliced garlic cloves, the tomatoes and the wine. Stir-fry for 3 minutes, until the wine has been absorbed.

4 Drain the pasta when ready and toss with the parsley, extra-virgin olive oil and the bottarga. Add the tomato sauce and toss again.

5 Top with the crema and serve immediately.

Although this dish suits the firm stubbiness of maccheroni well, you can also make a version with spaghetti and dress it with garlic-infused oil instead of the crema.

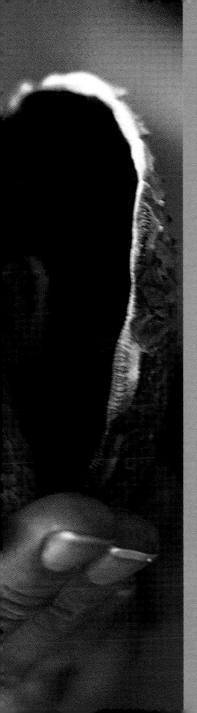

CHAPTER

4

pasta
everyday

As I have said several times elsewhere in this book, like most Italians I don't regard it as being a proper day unless I've had at least one plate of pasta. Everyday pasta is family fare, using the least expensive ingredients, such as seasonal vegetables and pulses. Flavouring ingredients like chillies and dried porcini also feature quite often, as they go a long way and deliver plenty of punch for pennies. Do not stint on buying the best and most flavourful oil, butter and cheese – as well, obviously, as good, tasty (made-in-Italy) pasta!

Pasta & peas

SERVES 2

2 tbsp olive oil

1 small onion, finely chopped

175g/6oz shelled fresh peas

600ml/1pint vegetable stock,
  preferably home-made

150g/5oz pappardelle

sea salt and freshly ground black pepper

handful of torn fresh basil leaves

lashings of freshly grated Parmesan cheese

1 Heat the oil in a medium saucepan, add the onion and fry until soft.

2 Add the peas and stock, and cook for 10 minutes until the peas are soft.

3 Add the pasta, broken up into pieces, with some salt and pepper to taste. Cook for about 12 minutes until the pasta is al dente, i.e. tender but still firm to the bite (it will absorb some of the stock).

4 Serve sprinkled with basil and Parmesan cheese.

To eat this at its best, use fresh new-season peas when they are sweet and tender.

Pasta with green vegetable sauce

SERVES 4

2 carrots
1 courgette
85g/3oz French beans
1 small leek
2 ripe Italian plum tomatoes
1 handful of flat-leaf parsley

350g/12oz pasta of your choice
sea salt and freshly ground black pepper
25g/1oz butter
3 tbsp extra-virgin olive oil
½ tsp sugar
115g/4oz fresh peas

1 Dice the carrots and the courgette finely. Top and tail the French beans, then cut into 2cm/¾in lengths. Slice the leek thinly. Peel and dice the tomatoes. Chop the parsley and set aside.

2 Cook the pasta in a pan of salted boiling water until al dente, i.e. just tender but still firm to the bite.

3 Melt the butter with the oil in a medium-sized saucepan. When the mixture sizzles, add the prepared leek and carrots. Sprinkle the sugar over and fry, stirring frequently, for about 5 minutes.

4 Stir in the courgettes, French beans, peas and plenty of salt and pepper. Cover and cook over a low-to-medium heat, stirring occasionally, for 5–8 minutes, until the vegetables are tender.

5 Stir in the parsley and chopped plum tomatoes, and adjust the seasoning to taste. Serve at once, tossed with the freshly cooked pasta.

Spaghetti with mushrooms

SERVES 4

15g/½oz dried porcini mushrooms
175ml/6fl oz warm water
3 tbsp olive oil
2 garlic cloves, finely chopped
handful of flat-leaf parsley, roughly
  chopped
2 large pieces of drained sun-dried tomato
  in olive oil, sliced into thin strips

125ml/4fl oz dry white wine
225g/8oz chestnut mushrooms, thinly sliced
450ml/¾ pint vegetable stock
350g/12oz spaghetti
sea salt and freshly ground black pepper
handful of mixed chopped rocket and
  parsley, to garnish

1 Put the dried porcini mushrooms in a bowl, pour the warm water over and leave to soak for 15–20 minutes. Tip into a fine sieve set over a bowl and squeeze the porcini with your hands to release as much liquid as possible. Reserve the strained soaking liquid. Chop the porcini finely.

2 Heat the oil and cook the garlic, parsley, sun-dried tomato strips and porcini over a low heat, stirring frequently, for about 5 minutes.

3 Stir in the wine, simmer for a few minutes until reduced by half, then stir in the chestnut mushrooms. Pour in the stock and simmer, uncovered, for 15–20 minutes, until the liquid has reduced and the sauce is quite thick and rich.

4 While that simmers, cook the pasta in plenty of boiling salted water until al dente, i.e. tender but still firm to the bite.

5 Taste the mushroom sauce and adjust the seasoning if necessary. Drain the cooked pasta, reserving a little of the cooking liquid, and tip it into a warmed large bowl. Add the mushroom sauce and toss well, thinning the sauce if necessary with some of the pasta cooking water.

6 Serve immediately, sprinkled liberally with chopped rocket and parsley.

To turn this into a special-occasion treat,
use mixed wild mushrooms, like fresh porcini
(ceps), chanterelles and morels.

Macaroni with broccoli & cauliflower

SERVES 4

175g/6oz cauliflower florets, cut into
   small sprigs
sea salt and freshly ground black pepper
175g/6oz broccoli florets, cut into small
   sprigs
350g/12oz short-cut macaroni
3 tbsp olive oil

1 onion, finely chopped
3 tbsp pine nuts
1 large pinch of saffron powder, dissolved
   in 1 tbsp warm water
1 tbsp raisins (optional)
2 tbsp sun-dried tomato paste
4 marinated anchovies, chopped, plus extra
   to serve (optional)

1 Cook the cauliflower in a large saucepan of boiling salted water for 3 minutes. Add the broccoli and boil both together for another 2 minutes. Remove the vegetables from the pan with a large slotted spoon and set aside.

2 Add the pasta to the vegetable cooking water and bring back to the boil. Cook the pasta until al dente, i.e. tender but still firm to the bite.

3 Meanwhile, heat the olive oil in a large skillet or saucepan, add the finely chopped onion and cook over a low-to-medium heat, stirring frequently, for about 2–3 minutes, until light golden.

4 Add the pine nuts, the cooked broccoli and cauliflower, the saffron water, raisins if using, the sun-dried tomato paste and a couple of ladlefuls of the pasta cooking water until the vegetable mixture has the consistency of a sauce. Finally season with plenty of pepper. Stir well.

5 Cook for 1–2 minute(s), then add the chopped anchovies.

6 Drain the cooked pasta and tip it into the vegetable mixture. Toss well, then taste and adjust the seasoning if necessary.

7 Serve the pasta immediately. You may like to add 1 or 2 whole anchovies on top of each serving.

Country-style rigatoni

SERVES 4

350g/12oz rigatoni or other pasta shape
sea salt and freshly ground black pepper
2 tender young courgettes
1 red onion
1 celery stalk
8 stoned olives
4 sun-dried tomatoes

115g/4oz Gorgonzola cheese
3 tbsp olive oil
1 garlic clove, crushed
glass of white wine
large handful of fresh basil leaves
freshly grated Parmesan cheese, to serve

1 Cook the pasta in a large pan of boiling salted water for about 10 minutes until al dente, i.e. just tender but still firm to the bite.

2 While the pasta cooks, chop the courgettes into julienne strips. Finely chop the onion and celery. Roughly chop the olives and chop the tomatoes. Cut the gorgonzola cheese into cubes.

3 Steam the courgette strips for 2 minutes.

4 In a medium saucepan, heat the oil and fry the onion for about 5 minutes until soft. Add the celery, garlic and wine and simmer for 6 minutes.

5 Add the courgette strips, olives, tomatoes, cubed cheese, basil, and salt and pepper to taste, and stir together.

6 Drain the cooked pasta, add the sauce and toss together. Adjust the seasoning to taste and serve immediately with Parmesan cheese.

Rigatoni are large pasta tubes which are ribbed on the outside. Their size and shape suit strongly flavoured sauces well.

This sauce is more usually served with plain white pasta. The red, green and white make it tricolore, the colours of the Italian flag.

Green tagliatelle
with fresh pea sauce

SERVES 4

1 tbsp olive oil

5–6 rindless rashers of streaky bacon,
  cut into strips

400g/14oz can of chopped Italian plum
  tomatoes

sea salt and freshly ground black pepper

350g/12oz dried tagliatelle verde

225g/8oz peas, preferably freshly shelled
  or frozen at a pinch

50g/2oz mascarpone cheese

few basil leaves, freshly torn, plus more
  whole leaves, to garnish

freshly grated Parmesan cheese

1 Heat the oil in a medium saucepan and add the bacon. Cook over a low heat, stirring frequently, for 5–7 minutes.

2 Add the tomatoes and 4 tablespoons of water with salt and pepper to taste. Bring to the boil, lower the heat, cover and simmer gently for about 15 minutes, stirring from time to time.

3 Meanwhile, cook the pasta in boiling salted water until al dente, i.e. tender but still firm to the bite.

4 Add the peas to the tomato sauce, stir well to mix and bring to the boil. Cover the pan and cook for 5–8 minutes, until the peas are cooked and the sauce is quite thick. Taste and adjust the seasoning if necessary.

5 Turn off the heat under the pan and add the mascarpone and basil. Mix well. Cover the pan and leave to stand for 1–2 minutes.

6 Drain the pasta and tip it into a warmed bowl. Pour the sauce over the pasta and toss well.

7 Serve immediately, garnished with basil leaves, and hand round some grated Parmesan separately.

Brandelli with aubergine & courgette

SERVES 4

200g/7oz aubergine
sea salt and freshly ground black pepper
350g/12oz brandelli
2 medium carrots
2 small courgettes
1 large onion
4 tbsp olive oil
2 garlic cloves, crushed
1 tbsp chopped fresh rosemary
100ml/3½fl oz red wine
85g/3oz freshly grated Pecorino cheese

1 Peel the aubergine and chop the flesh into matchsticks. Put in a bowl and sprinkle with salt. Place a plate on top and weigh down. Leave for 20 minutes.

2 Toward the end of this time, cook the pasta in a large saucepan of boiling salted water for about 12 minutes until al dente, i.e. just tender but still firm to the bite.

3 While the pasta cooks, cut the carrots and courgettes into matchsticks. Finely chop the onion. Rinse the aubergine matchsticks and pat dry.

4 Heat the olive oil in a saucepan, add the carrot, courgette and aubergine matchsticks and fry until golden. Add the onion and fry until coloured, then add the garlic and rosemary. Lower the heat and add the wine, with salt and pepper to taste. Simmer, covered, for 5 minutes.

5 Drain the cooked pasta and toss into the sauce so it is all covered. Serve sprinkled with the Pecorino cheese.

If the crinkled squares of brandelli are not available, you could use pappardelle.

Stuffed giant pasta shells

SERVES 2

12 giant pasta shells
salt and freshly ground black pepper
350g/12oz broccoli florets
50g/2oz pine nuts

225g/8oz Dolcelatte cheese
1 garlic clove, crushed
small handful of finely snipped fresh chives
a little extra-virgin olive oil
freshly grated Parmesan cheese, to serve

1 Cook the pasta shells in a large pan of boiling salted water for about 10 minutes until al dente, i.e. just tender but still firm to the bite.

2 While the pasta cooks, steam the broccoli florets for about 8 minutes until tender.

3 Toast the pine nuts on a sheet of foil under the grill, turning them frequently.

4 Put the steamed broccoli, Dolcelatte, pine nuts, garlic and chives in a bowl. Season with salt and pepper to taste and mix together.

5 Drain the pasta and toss it in a little olive oil to prevent the shells from sticking together. While still warm, stuff them with the filling.

6 Place the stuffed pasta shells in a greased shallow ovenproof serving dish, sprinkle over the Parmesan cheese and grill until bubbling. Serve immediately.

These large pasta shells suit a whole range of different stuffings – try roasted peppers and tomatoes, or ham and mushrooms with cheese.

Try this dish with roast pumpkin. Replace the parsley and oregano with fresh sage leaves.

Conchiglie with roasted vegetables

SERVES 4

1 red pepper, deseeded and cut into
  1cm/½ in squares
1 yellow pepper, deseeded and cut into
  1cm/½ in squares
1 small aubergine, roughly diced
2 courgettes, roughly diced
5 tbsp extra-virgin olive oil
handful of chopped fresh flat-leaf parsley

1 tsp dried oregano
sea salt and freshly ground black pepper
250g/9oz cherry tomatoes, preferably on the
  vine, cut in half
2 garlic cloves, roughly chopped
350g/12oz conchiglie (pasta shells)
marjoram flowers or oregano
  flowers, to garnish (optional)

1 Preheat the oven to 190°C/375°F/Gas 5. Rinse the prepared peppers, aubergine and courgettes under running water. Drain, then lay the vegetables in a roasting tin.

2 Pour 3 tablespoons of the olive oil all over the vegetables and sprinkle with the fresh and dried herbs. Season to taste and stir well. Roast for about 30 minutes, stirring 2 or 3 times.

3 Stir the halved tomatoes and chopped garlic into the vegetable mixture and then roast for 20 minutes more, again stirring once or twice.

4 Meanwhile, cook the pasta in boiling salted water until al dente, i.e. tender but still firm to the bite.

5 Drain the cooked pasta and tip it into a warmed bowl. Add the roasted vegetables and the remaining oil, and toss well.

6 Serve the pasta and vegetables hot in warmed bowls, sprinkling each portion well with a few herb flowers if you have them.

Rigatoni with garlic, chilli & mushrooms

SERVES 4

2 whole garlic bulbs, plus 1 extra garlic
   clove, crushed
2 tbsp olive oil, plus extra to drizzle
1 red chilli

300g/10oz flat mushrooms
350g/12oz rigatoni
sea salt and freshly ground black pepper
150ml/¼ pint double cream
freshly grated Parmesan cheese to serve

1 Preheat the oven to 200°C/400°F/Gas 6. Slice the tops off the whole garlic bulbs and put in a roasting tin. Drizzle with a little oil and roast in the oven for 30 minutes, turning after 15 minutes. They will become golden and papery on the outside. Leave to cool slightly.

2 Finely chop the chilli, discarding the seeds. Roughly chop the mushrooms. Heat the olive oil in a frying pan, add the mushrooms and fry for 8 minutes. Add the chilli and the crushed garlic, and cook for a further 4 minutes.

3 Meanwhile, cook the pasta in boiling salted water until al dente, i.e. tender but still firm to the bite.

4 While the pasta is cooking, squeeze the roasted garlic cloves like toothpaste from a tube to extract the garlic pulp from each clove. Add the pulp to the mushroom mixture. Stir in the cream and add salt and pepper.

5 Drain the cooked pasta and pour over the sauce. Serve with the cheese.

Roasting garlic gives it an entirely different and much more complex flavour.

Spaghetti with anchovies & olives

SERVES 4

3 tbsp olive oil

1 large red pepper, deseeded and chopped

1 small aubergine, finely chopped

1 onion, finely chopped

8 ripe Italian plum tomatoes, skinned, deseeded and finely chopped

2 garlic cloves, finely chopped

125ml/4fl oz dry red wine

handful of mixed basil, flat-leaf parsley and rosemary

sea salt and freshly ground black pepper

350g/12oz dried spaghetti

50g/2oz canned anchovies, roughly chopped, plus extra to garnish

12 pitted black olives

1–2 tbsp salt-packed capers, to taste

1 Heat the oil in a saucepan and add all the finely chopped vegetables and garlic. Cook gently, stirring frequently, for 10–15 minutes, until the vegetables are soft.

2 Pour in the wine and 125ml/4fl oz water. Add the fresh herbs and pepper to taste. Bring to the boil. Lower the heat and simmer, stirring occasionally, for 10–15 minutes.

3 Meanwhile, cook the pasta in a large pan of salted boiling water until al dente, i.e. just tender but still firm to the bite.

4 Add the chopped anchovies, olives and capers to the sauce. Heat through for a few minutes, taste and adjust the seasoning.

5 Drain the pasta and tip it into a large warmed bowl. Pour the sauce over the pasta, toss well and serve immediately, garnished with the whole anchovies.

Chitarra with sardines & breadcrumbs

SERVES 4
8 filleted sardines
4 tbsp olive oil
sea salt and freshly ground black pepper
400g/14oz chitarra pasta

2 garlic cloves, crushed
2 good handfuls of fresh herbs, such as
   parsley, basil, thyme, plus more parsley
   for garnish
115g/4oz breadcrumbs, toasted

1 Preheat the grill to medium. Brush the sardines with 2 tablespoons of oil and season. Grill for 8 minutes on each side, then allow to cool.

2 Cook the pasta in a pan of salted boiling water until al dente, i.e. just tender but still firm to the bite.

3 Heat the remaining oil in a small pan, add the garlic and fry gently, being careful not to allow it to colour. Break up the sardines when cool enough to handle and add with the herbs to the pasta. Toss well and add the breadcrumbs.

4 Serve immediately in warmed bowls, topped with parsley to garnish.

Chitarra resembles spaghetti but is square in section. You could use spaghetti or linguine as an alternative.

Pasta in parcels with tuna & potatoes

SERVES 4

250g/9oz tuna steak, chopped into
2cm/¾in cubes
1 glass of white wine
2 garlic cloves, finely chopped
grated zest of 1 lemon
2 sprigs of rosemary, broken into pieces
sea salt and freshly ground black pepper

8 new potatoes (preferably Italian),
peeled and cut into small dice
12 ripe plum tomatoes (preferably Italian),
deseeded and roughly chopped
handful of flat-leaf parsley, chopped,
plus more to serve
350g/12oz spaghetti
2 tbsp olive oil

1 Place the tuna in a bowl with the wine, garlic, lemon zest, rosemary and some seasoning. Leave to marinate for 30 minutes. Preheat the oven to 200°C/400°F/Gas 6.

2 Towards the end of marinating time, cook the potato dice in boiling salted water for 6 minutes until tender and drain. Combine with the tomatoes and parsley.

3 At the same time, half-cook the spaghetti (use just over half the time suggested on the packet). Drain well.

4 In a large frying pan, heat the oil until hot, add the tuna with its marinade and fry very quickly for 6 minutes. Combine with the spaghetti, tomatoes and potato.

5 Mix the contents of the frying pan with the spaghetti, tomatoes and potato. Prepare 4 parcels with parchment paper, add one-quarter of the mixture to each and fold up loosely like an envelope. Fold in the edges and then fold over the top carefully to seal completely.

6 Place in the preheated oven for 7 minutes. Serve at once, slashing the bags at the table and sprinkling with more parsley.

Instead of chicken, try using well-trimmed chicken livers.

Farfalle with chicken & cherry tomatoes

SERVES 4

350g/12oz skinless chicken breast fillets,
   cut into bite-sized pieces

4 tbsp Italian dry vermouth

2 tsp chopped fresh rosemary, plus 4 fresh
   rosemary sprigs to garnish

sea salt and freshly ground black pepper

1 tbsp olive oil

1 onion, finely chopped

85g/3oz piece of Italian salami, diced

275g/10oz dried farfalle

1 tbsp balsamic vinegar

400g/14oz can of Italian cherry tomatoes

good pinch of crushed dried red chillies

1 Put the pieces of chicken in a large bowl, pour over the dry vermouth and sprinkle with half the chopped rosemary and salt and pepper to taste. Stir well and set aside.

2 Heat the oil in a large saucepan, add the onion and salami, and fry over a medium heat for about 5 minutes, stirring frequently.

3 Meanwhile, cook the pasta in a large pan of salted boiling water until al dente, i.e. just tender but still firm to the bite.

4 Add the chicken and vermouth to the onion and salami, increase the heat to high and fry for 3 minutes, or until the chicken is white on all sides. Sprinkle the vinegar over the chicken. Add the cherry tomatoes and dried chillies, stir well and simmer for a few minutes more. Taste the sauce and adjust the seasoning if necessary.

5 Drain the pasta and tip it into the sauce. Add the remaining chopped rosemary and toss to mix the pasta and sauce together. Serve immediately, in warmed bowls garnished with rosemary sprigs.

Penne with chicken, broccoli & cheese

SERVES 4

115g/4oz broccoli, divided into tiny florets
sea salt and freshly ground black pepper
50g/2oz unsalted butter
2 skinless chicken breast fillets, cut into
   thin strips
2 garlic cloves, crushed

400g/14oz dried penne
125ml/4fl oz dry white wine
200ml/7fl oz double cream
85g/3oz Gorgonzola cheese, rind removed
   and cut into small dice
freshly grated Parmesan cheese, to serve

1 Plunge the broccoli into a saucepan of boiling salted water. Bring back to the boil and boil for 2 minutes, then drain in a colander and refresh in cold water. Shake well to remove surplus water and set aside to drain completely.

2 Melt the butter in a large saucepan, add the chicken and garlic with salt and pepper to taste, and stir well. Fry over a medium heat for 3 minutes or until the chicken becomes white.

3 Meanwhile, cook the pasta in a large pan of salted boiling water until al dente, i.e. just tender but still firm to the bite.

4 Pour the wine and cream over the chicken mixture in the saucepan and stir well to mix. Simmer, stirring occasionally, for about 5 minutes until the sauce has reduced and thickened. Add the broccoli, then increase the heat and toss to heat it through. Mix with the chicken. Taste and adjust the seasoning if necessary.

5 Drain the pasta and tip it into the sauce. Add the Gorgonzola and toss well. Serve with grated Parmesan.

For an even more substantial dish, try adding some sliced pancetta and chopped fresh sage to the chicken.

Eliche with sausage & radicchio

SERVES 4

2 tbsp olive oil
1 onion, finely chopped
200g/7oz Italian pure pork sausage
175ml/6fl oz passata

6 tbsp dry white wine
sea salt and freshly ground black pepper
350g/12oz dried eliche
50g/2oz radicchio leaves

1 Heat the olive oil in a large deep saucepan, add the finely chopped onion and cook over a low heat, stirring frequently, for about 5 minutes until softened.

2 Cut the sausage into bite-sized chunks and add to the pan. Stir to mix with the oil and onion and continue to fry the mixture, increasing the heat if necessary, until the sausage is well browned all over.

3 Stir in the passata, then sprinkle in the wine with salt and pepper to taste. Simmer over a low heat, stirring occasionally, for 10–12 minutes.

4 Meanwhile, cook the pasta in a large pan of salted boiling water until al dente, i.e. just tender but still firm to the bite.

5 Just before draining the pasta, add a ladleful or two of the cooking water to the sausage sauce and stir well. Taste the sauce and adjust the seasoning if necessary. Slice the radicchio leaves thinly.

6 Drain the cooked pasta and tip it into the pan of sausage sauce. Add the shredded radicchio and toss well to combine everything together. Serve immediately.

Eliche are pasta spirals that look like propellers or screw-threads. As an alternative, you could use fusilli.

Bucatini with sausage & pancetta

SERVES 4

115g/4oz pork sausage meat
400g/14oz can of Italian plum tomatoes
1 tbsp olive oil
1 garlic clove, crushed
115g/4oz pancetta or rindless streaky
    bacon, roughly chopped

handful of chopped fresh flat-leaf parsley
sea salt and freshly ground black pepper
400g/14oz dried bucatini
4–5 tbsp double cream
2 egg yolks

1 Remove any skin from the sausage meat and break the meat up roughly with a knife. Purée the tomatoes in a food processor or blender.

2 Heat the oil in a medium-sized saucepan, add the garlic and fry over a low heat for 1–2 minutes. Remove the garlic with a slotted spoon and discard it.

3 Add the sausage meat and pancetta or bacon to the pan, and cook over a medium heat for 3–4 minutes. Stir constantly using a wooden spoon to break up the sausage meat – it will become brown and look crumbly.

4 Add the puréed tomatoes to the pan with half the parsley and salt and pepper to taste. Stir well and bring to the boil, scraping up any sediment that has stuck to the bottom of the pan. Lower the heat, cover and simmer for 20 minutes, stirring from time-to-time. Taste and adjust the seasoning, if necessary.

5 Meanwhile, cook the pasta in boiling salted water until al dente, i.e. tender but still firm to the bite.

6 Put the cream and egg yolks in a warmed large bowl and mix with a fork, seasoning with salt and pepper. As soon as the pasta is cooked, drain it well and add to the bowl of cream mixture. Toss until the pasta is coated, then pour the sausage meat sauce over the pasta and toss again.

7 Serve immediately in warmed bowls, sprinkled with the remaining parsley.

For authenticity, source **salsiccia a metro**, a pure pork sausage sold by the metre at good Italian delicatessens.

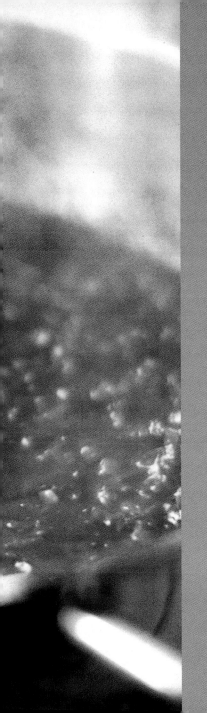

CHAPTER

pasta
light &
healthy

Pasta itself is basically high in complex carbohydrates and low in fat; it is only the sauces that might introduce high levels of fats. What is more, the primary fat in pasta sauces tends to be healthy olive oil. You can also, as in this chapter, make a point of including more foods containing plant chemicals that are positively good for you, like broccoli and – of course – tomatoes, which both help to protect against cancer and heart disease.

Spaghetti with tiny tomatoes

SERVES 2

450g/1lb cherry tomatoes
3 large garlic cloves, cut into slivers
sea salt and freshly ground black pepper
200g/7oz spaghetti
1 small hot chilli pepper, deseeded and
    chopped (optional)

1 tbsp olive oil for the chilli, if necessary
handful of fresh basil, torn
2 tbsp extra-virgin olive oil
freshly grated Parmesan cheese, to serve

1 Preheat the oven to 150°C/300°F/Gas 2. Cut the tomatoes in half and put on a baking sheet. Place a sliver of garlic on top of each, followed by a sprinkling of salt. Bake for 1¼ hours until dry but still squashy.

2 Cook the pasta in a large pan of boiling salted water for about 10 minutes until al dente, i.e. just tender but still firm to the bite. If using the chilli, fry it in olive oil just long enough to colour it, then remove it from the heat.

3 Drain the pasta and stir in the tomatoes, chilli if using, basil and extra-virgin olive oil, with salt and pepper to taste.

4 Serve sprinkled with the cheese.

The last person to be served is the luckiest,
as they get the most sauce.

Conchiglie with fennel & tomato sauce

SERVES 4

2 medium fennel bulbs
3 tbsp olive oil
1 garlic clove
400g/14oz can chopped tomatoes

grated zest of 1 unwaxed lemon
handful of mint, chopped
350g/12oz conchiglie (pasta shells)
sea salt and freshly ground black pepper
freshly grated Parmesan cheese, to serve

1 Preheat the oven to 200°C/400°F/Gas 6.

2 Remove the fennel's tough outer leaves and tough core, and wash well. Cut into lengths and steam or cook in boiling water for 7–8 minutes until tender. Transfer to a roasting tin and drizzle over a tablespoon of olive oil. Roast in the oven for 15 minutes until golden.

3 Meanwhile, crush the garlic clove. Heat the remaining olive oil in a saucepan, add the garlic and fry gently until softened. Add the tomatoes, lemon zest and chopped mint, and cook gently for 25 minutes.

4 Towards the end of this time, cook the pasta in boiling salted water until al dente, i.e. just tender but still firm to the bite.

5 Chop the roast fennel into small pieces and add to the sauce. Season well with salt and pepper and heat gently.

6 Drain the cooked pasta and toss with the sauce. Serve hot, with plenty of grated Parmesan cheese.

Pasta Vesuvius

SERVES 2

4 tomatoes
200g/7oz fettuccine
sea salt and freshly ground black pepper
25g/1oz stoned black or green olives
25g/1oz capers, well rinsed
1 tbsp olive oil
1 garlic clove, crushed

½ dried chilli, deseeded and chopped
handful of flat-leaf parsley, finely chopped,
   plus more whole sprigs, to garnish
handful of fresh mint, finely chopped,
   plus more whole sprigs, to garnish
2 tbsp mascarpone cheese or single cream
2 tsp freshly grated Parmesan cheese

1 Put the tomatoes in a bowl, cover with boiling water for about 40 seconds then plunge into cold water. Using a sharp knife, peel off the skins and chop the flesh, discarding the seeds.

2 Cook the pasta in a large saucepan of boiling salted water for 10 minutes until al dente, i.e. just tender but still firm to the bite.

3 Meanwhile, finely chop the olives and capers. Heat the oil in a saucepan and fry the garlic until softened. Add the olives, capers, tomatoes, chilli, parsley and mint, and fry gently for about 5 minutes. Add the mascarpone cheese. Season with salt and pepper to taste.

4 Drain the pasta, add to the pan and toss together with grated Parmesan cheese. Garnish with sprigs of fresh mint and parsley to serve.

For a special occasion, when you are not so concerned with fat and calories, add a little double cream after the mascarpone.

Trenette with pesto, beans & potatoes

SERVES 2
2 potatoes (about 250g/9oz)
100g/3½oz French beans
sea salt and freshly ground black pepper
350g/12oz dried trenette

FOR THE PESTO
very generous handful of fresh basil leaves

2 garlic cloves, thinly sliced
1½ tbsp pine nuts
3 tbsp freshly grated Parmesan cheese,
  plus extra to serve
2 tbsp freshly grated Pecorino cheese
4 tbsp extra-virgin olive oil
pinch of salt

1 First make the pesto: put the basil leaves, garlic, pine nuts and cheeses in a food processor and blend for 5 seconds. Add half of the oil and a pinch of salt and blend for 5 seconds more. Stop the machine, remove the lid and scrape down the side of the bowl. Add the remaining oil and blend for 5–10 seconds.

2 Cut the potatoes in half lengthays, then cut each half across into 5mm/¼in thick slices. Cut the beans into 2cm/¾in pieces. Plunge the potatoes and beans into a large saucepan of salted boiling water and boil, uncovered, for 5 minutes.

3 Add the pasta, bring the water back to the boil, stir well and cook for 5–7 minutes or until the pasta is al dente, i.e. just tender but still firm to the bite.

4 Meanwhile, put the pesto in a large bowl and add 3–4 tablespoons of the water used for cooking the pasta. Mix well.

5 Drain the pasta and vegetables, add to the pesto and toss well. Serve immediately on warmed plates with extra grated Parmesan and Pecorino handed round separately.

Trenette is the traditional Ligurian pasta that is served with pesto. If you find it difficult to obtain, use bavette or linguine instead.

Some of the best broccoli is grown in the southern regions of Italy, hence its other name, calabrese – from Calabria.

Pasta with broccoli

SERVES 2

200g/7oz ditali (short macaroni)
sea salt and freshly ground black pepper
375g/13oz broccoli
3–4 bay leaves
50g/2oz stoned green olives

2 tbsp olive oil
1 garlic clove, finely chopped
50g/2oz ground almonds
3 tbsp freshly toasted breadcrumbs
extra-virgin olive oil, to serve
freshly grated Parmesan cheese, to serve

1 Cook the pasta in a large saucepan of boiling salted water for about 10 minutes until al dente, i.e. just tender but still firm to the bite.

2 While the pasta is cooking, cut the broccoli into florets and steam with the bay leaves for about 6 minutes until tender.

3 While the pasta and broccoli are cooking, finely chop the olives. Heat the oil and garlic in a frying pan, then add the olives and ground almonds, and heat very gently, adding a tablespoon of water.

4 Drain the cooked pasta, toss in the broccoli, olive and almond mixture and the breadcrumbs. Mix together. Drizzle over some extra-virgin olive oil and serve with grated Parmesan cheese.

Orecchiette
with rocket

SERVES 4

3 tbsp olive oil

1 small onion, finely chopped

350g/12oz chopped plum tomatoes or passata

½ tsp dried oregano

pinch of chilli flakes

about 2 tbsp white wine (optional)

sea salt and freshly ground black pepper

350g/12oz dried orecchiette

2 garlic cloves, finely chopped

150g/5oz rocket leaves, stalks removed and leaves shredded

45g/1½oz ricotta cheese

freshly grated Pecorino cheese, to serve

1 Heat 1 tablespoon of the olive oil in a medium-sized saucepan, add half the finely chopped onion and cook gently, stirring frequently, for about 5 minutes until softened. Add the tomatoes, oregano and chilli flakes to the onion, pour over the wine if using and season with a little salt and pepper to taste. Cover the pan and simmer for about 15 minutes, stirring occasionally.

2 Meanwhile, cook the pasta in a pan of boiling salted water for about 15 minutes until al dente, i.e. just tender but still firm to the bite.

3 Heat the remaining oil in a large saucepan, add the rest of the onion and the garlic. Fry for 2–3 minutes, stirring occasionally. Add the rocket, toss over the heat for about 2 minutes until wilted, then stir in the tomato sauce and the ricotta. Mix well.

4 Drain the pasta, add to the pan of sauce and toss to mix. Taste and adjust the seasoning if necessary. Serve immediately in warmed bowls with grated Pecorino handed round separately.

Orecchiette (little ears) from Puglia are a special type of pasta with a chewy texture. You could use conchiglie instead.

If you can't find turnip tops, use Swiss chard or spinach instead.

Linguine with clams & turnip tops

SERVES 4

625g/1½lb Venus clams or vongole verace
a little plain flour
2 tbsp olive oil
2 leeks, thinly sliced
2 fresh bay leaves
1 garlic clove, crushed

200ml/7fl oz dry white wine
sea salt and freshly ground black pepper
350g/12oz linguine
350g/12oz turnip tops (cime di rape),
    finely chopped
3 tbsp roughly chopped flat-leaf parsley

1 Keep the clams submerged in water with a little added plain flour (this helps to plump them up and purge them of any dirt). Discard any open ones that don't close when they are tapped.

2 Heat the oil in a large saucepan, add the leeks and bay leaves, and fry over a high heat until the leeks have some colour. Add the garlic and wine, season with salt and pepper to taste, and the drained clams. Cover and cook over a medium-high heat for about 6 minutes, until all the clams open (discard any that don't).

3 At the same time, cook the linguine in a large saucepan of boiling salted water until al dente, i.e. just tender but still firm to the bite. Drain.

4 Remove the lid from the clam pan and throw in the rape and the chard or spinach. Stir. Add the drained linguine and the parsley. Mix well, adjust the seasoning and serve immediately.

Penne with prawns & artichokes

SERVES 4

juice of 1 lemon

4 baby globe artichokes, preferably with
    good long stalks

3 tbsp olive oil

2 garlic cloves, crushed

handful of chopped fresh mint

handful of chopped fresh flat-leaf parsley

sea salt and freshly ground black pepper

350g/12oz dried penne

16 peeled cooked king or tiger prawns,
    preferably with their tail shells attached

2 tbsp fruity fine extra-virgin olive oil

1 Have ready a large pan of cold water to which you have added the lemon juice.
To prepare the artichokes, cut off most of the stalks, if any, and cut across the tops
of the leaves. Peel off and discard any tough or discoloured outer leaves. Cut the
artichokes lengthways into quarters and remove any hairy chokes from their centres.
Put the pieces of artichoke in the pan of acidulated water to help prevent browning.
Bring to the boil and simmer gently for about 10 minutes.

2 Drain the pieces of artichoke and pat them dry. Heat the olive oil in a non-stick
frying pan and add the artichokes, the crushed garlic and half the mint and parsley
to the pan. Season with plenty of salt and pepper, and cook over a low heat, stirring
frequently, for about 3–4 minutes or until the artichokes are just tender.

3 Meanwhile, cook the pasta in a large pan of boiling salted water until al dente,
i.e. just tender but still firm to the bite.

4 Add the prawns to the artichokes and stir well to mix. Heat through over a gentle
heat for 2 minutes.

5 Drain the cooked pasta and tip into a warmed bowl. Dress with the extra-virgin
olive oil, spoon the artichoke mixture over the pasta and toss to combine.

6 Serve immediately, sprinkled with the remaining mint and parsley.

Orecchiette with anchovies & broccoli

SERVES 4

350g/12oz broccoli florets
sea salt and freshly ground black pepper
25g/1oz pine nuts
350g/12oz dried orecchiette

2 tbsp olive oil
1 small red onion, thinly sliced
50g/2oz jar of anchovies in olive oil, drained
1 garlic clove crushed
25g/1oz freshly grated Pecorino cheese

1 Break the broccoli florets into small sprigs and cut off the stalks. Chop or slice large stalks. Cook the broccoli florets and stalks in a saucepan of boiling salted water for 2 minutes, then drain and refresh in cold water. Leave to drain on kitchen paper.

2 Put the pine nuts in a dry nonstick frying pan and toss over a low-to-medium heat for 1–2 minutes until the nuts are lightly toasted. Remove and set aside.

3 Cook the pasta in a large pan of boiling salted water until al dente, i.e. just tender but still firm to the bite.

4 Meanwhile, heat the oil in a frying pan, add the onion and fry gently, stirring often, for about 5 minutes until softened. Add the anchovies, followed by the garlic, and cook over a medium heat until the anchovies break down to a paste. Add the broccoli and plenty of pepper and toss over the heat for a minute or two until the broccoli is hot. Taste and adjust the seasoning.

5 Drain the pasta and tip into a warm bowl. Add the broccoli mixture and grated Pecorino. Toss well. Sprinkle with pine nuts and serve immediately in warmed bowls.

Orecchiette (little ears) from Puglia are a special type of pasta with a chewy texture. You could use conchiglie instead.

Bucatini with sardines & fennel

SERVES 4
375g/13oz bucatini

FOR THE SAUCE
1 onion, finely chopped
2 garlic cloves, peeled and crushed
3 tbsp olive oil
 handful of fennel fronds, finely chopped
400g/14oz canned chopped tomatoes
1 dsp currants
100g/3½oz pine nuts

1 tsp dried chilli flakes
sea salt
500g/1lb 2oz fresh sardine fillets, rinsed

FOR THE PASTA TOPPING
100g/3½oz fresh breadcrumbs
2 tbsp olive oil
4 ripe tomatoes, deseeded and chopped
1 garlic clove, peeled and crushed
pinch of dried chilli flakes
handful of flat-leaf parsley leaves, chopped

1 First make the sauce: sauté the onion and garlic in the olive oil. Add the fennel, tomatoes, currants, pine nuts, chilli and a little salt. Simmer, stirring occasionally, for 30 minutes. Add the sardines and cook for 12 minutes – they will break up.

2 Meanwhile, make the topping: toast the breadcrumbs in a frying pan, mixing in the olive oil, tomatoes, garlic, a little salt and the chilli. Stir constantly, without allowing the breadcrumbs to burn, until they are coloured and crunchy. Sprinkle with parsley.

3 Cook the pasta in a large pan of boiling salted water until al dente, i.e. just tender but still firm to the bite.

4 Drain the pasta, reserving a ladleful of the cooking water. Pour half of the sauce into the pan. Add the pasta and stir to coat completely. Pour into a serving dish and cover with the rest of the sauce, adding the reserved cooking water if needed to give enough sauce. Serve immediately with the breadcrumb topping.

Bucatini are the long hollow noodles, like slightly fatter spaghetti.

Instead of squid and peas, try adding chunks of roasted vegetables, such as courgettes, peppers or aubergines, to the tomato sauce.

Pasta pie with squid & peas

SERVES 4–6

350g/12oz dried conchiglie or rigatoni
about 6 medium squid, prepared
grated zest and juice of 1 unwaxed lemon
200g/7oz fresh peas
2 tbsp dry breadcrumbs

FOR THE TOMATO SAUCE

2 tbsp olive oil
1 small onion, finely chopped
400g/14oz canned chopped plum tomatoes

1 tbsp sun-dried tomato paste
handful of freshly chopped herbs
   (sage, thyme, rosemary and parsley)
sea salt and freshly ground black pepper

FOR THE WHITE SAUCE

25g/1oz unsalted butter
25g/1oz '00' plain Italian flour or plain flour
600ml/1 pint skimmed milk
1 egg

1 First make the tomato sauce: heat the olive oil in a large saucepan and cook the onion over a gentle heat, stirring, until softened. Stir in the tomatoes, then fill the empty can with water and add this to the tomato mixture with the tomato paste and herbs. And salt and pepper to taste. Simmer for 20 minutes.

2 Meanwhile, preheat the oven to 190°C/375°F/Gas 5. Cook the pasta in a large saucepan of boiling salted water until al dente, i.e. just tender but still firm to the bite.

3 Meanwhile, make the white sauce. Melt the butter in a pan, add the flour and cook, stirring, for 1 minute. Add the milk, a little at a time, whisking well after each addition. Bring to the boil and cook, stirring, until the sauce is smooth and thick. Season to taste, then remove the pan from the heat.

4 Chop the squid into rings and sauté in hot oil for about 4 minutes. Drain the pasta and tip into a baking dish. Add the squid, lemon zest and juice, and the peas to the tomato sauce. Adjust the seasoning and pour into the dish. Mix with the pasta.

5 Beat the egg into the white sauce, then pour the sauce over the pasta mixture. Separate the pasta with a fork so that the white sauce fills the gaps. Level the surface, sprinkle with breadcrumbs and bake for 15 minutes until golden brown and bubbly.

CHAPTER

6

pasta cook ahead

For busy people or those with large families,
it is always useful to be able to make tasty fresh
pasta sauces, like traditional Ligurian pesto
and its not-so-traditional but equally spirited
variations, in advance, when you have the time.
Also, when you have just that little bit more
time, you can conjure up some of the tasty baked
and stuffed pastas, such as ravioli, lasagne and
cannelloni. Many of these are actually all the
better for being made in advance, as the flavours
have a chance to mingle and develop.

Squares of pasta with pesto

SERVES 2

FOR THE PASTA

200g/7oz strong white unbleached flour,
  preferably Italian grade '00'
pinch of sea salt
2 large eggs
1 tbsp olive oil

FOR THE PESTO

1 garlic clove, crushed
25g/1oz pine nuts
pinch of sea salt
2 tbsp freshly grated Parmesan cheese,
  plus extra to serve
50g/2oz fresh basil leaves
5 tbsp fruity extra-virgin olive oil

1 Make the pasta dough as described on pages 10–13 and leave to rest in a cool place for about 30 minutes.

2 Roll out the pasta dough in a pasta machine (see pages 14–17). Alternatively, divide the dough into manageable pieces and cover the dough you are not working with. Take each piece of dough and, with the heel of your hand, press it out. Using a long, thin rolling pin and a little flour, gently roll out the dough as thinly as you can. Leave to dry on a clean tea towel for 30 minutes. Cut the pasta into 15cm/6in squares.

3 Make the pesto: using a pestle and mortar, pound the garlic, pine nuts and salt together. Add the cheese and basil, and continue to pound. Add the oil, a little at a time, and pound until you have a smooth paste.

4 Cook half the pasta squares in boiling salted water for 7 minutes until al dente, i.e. just tender but still firm to the bite. Drain and toss the pasta with some of the sauce, then serve hot with freshly grated Parmesan cheese. Cook and serve the rest in the same way.

As they are quite plain, you can also serve these pasta squares with the other pesto ideas on the following pages.

Tortellini with ricotta

SERVES 6

FOR THE PASTA

600g/1lb 5oz strong white unbleached flour,
preferably Italian '00' grade
pinch of sea salt
6 large eggs
1 tbsp olive oil
semolina, for sprinkling

FOR THE FILLING

150g/5oz freshly grated Parmesan cheese
150g/5oz ricotta
50g/2oz truffle condiment (a paste of
minced truffle, sometimes with porcini)
sea salt and freshly ground black pepper

TO FINISH

knob of unsalted butter
fresh basil leaves
more freshly grated Parmesan cheese

1 Make the pasta dough as described on pages 10–13 and leave to rest in a cool place for about 30 minutes.

2 Make the filling: mix together the Parmesan cheese, ricotta and truffle condiment, with salt and pepper to taste.

3 Roll out the dough in a pasta machine (see pages 14–17). Alternatively, divide the dough into manageable pieces and keep the dough covered when not being worked. Take one piece of dough and, with the heel of your hand, press it out. Using a long, thin rolling pin and a little flour, gently roll out the pasta to an even, almost paper-thin, sheet, sprinkling the surface with semolina. Cut the pasta into 10cm/4in squares.

4 Place a teaspoonful of filling in the centre of each square. Moisten the edges with water then fold one corner over to make a triangle, making sure there is little or no trapped air. Press the edges lightly together, bringing the corners of the triangle in towards another to make a circular shape. Lay the tortellini on baking sheets, sprinkle with semolina and leave to dry for 1 hour.

5 Put the tortellini in a large saucepan of boiling salted water and bring back to the boil. Reduce the heat and poach at a gentle simmer for 4–5 minutes until al dente, i.e. just tender but still firm to the bite. Drain and serve, dressed with a knob of butter and garnished with basil leaves, with extra Parmesan cheese served separately.

This sauce is not only good with pasta but also makes an excellent salad dressing or can be used to dress freshly steamed vegetables.

Red pepper pesto with penne rigate

SERVES 6

500g/1lb 2oz penne rigate (the ridged
  version of penne)
fresh basil leaves, to garnish

FOR THE PESTO

4 medium red peppers
65g/2¼oz ground almonds

zest of 1 unwaxed lemon, finely chopped
4 tbsp extra-virgin olive oil, plus a little
  more to finish
1 garlic clove, peeled
2 tsp balsamic vinegar
50g/2oz freshly grated Parmesan cheese
sea salt and freshly ground black pepper

1 To make the pesto: preheat the oven to 200°C/400°F/Gas 6. Put the peppers on a baking sheet and roast them in the preheated oven for 25 minutes, turning them once during cooking. They should become charred and deflated. Remove and leave to cool on a wire rack. This can be done a day ahead if that is easier.

2 When the peppers are cool, peel off the skin and remove the seeds. Try to save the precious juices from the peppers by holding them over a bowl as you do this.

3 Put the pepper flesh and juices, and all the other ingredients in the food processor and whiz until blended smooth and thick. Taste and adjust the seasoning if necessary.

4 Cook the pasta in a large pan of boiling salted water until al dente, i.e. just tender but still firm to the bite. Drain and toss the pasta with the sauce, then garnish with some basil leaves to serve.

Pansotti with cheese, herbs & walnut sauce

SERVES 6–8

½ quantity egg pasta (page 10–13)

handful of finely chopped parsley, plus
  some more sprigs for garnish

very small handful of finely chopped thyme

flour, for dusting

50g/2oz unsalted butter

freshly grated Parmesan cheese, to serve

FOR THE FILLING

250g/9oz ricotta cheese

150g/5oz freshly grated Parmesan cheese

large handful each of fresh basil leaves and
  flat-leaf parsley, finely chopped

few sprigs of fresh marjoram or oregano,
  leaves removed and finely chopped

1 garlic clove, crushed

1 small egg

sea salt and freshly ground black pepper

FOR THE WALNUT SAUCE

90g/3¼oz shelled fresh walnuts

1 garlic clove

4 tbsp extra-virgin olive oil

125ml/4fl oz double cream

1 Make the pasta as described on pages 10–13, but adding the herbs to the well as you mix the ingredients. Leave to rest in a cool place for at least 30 minutes.

2 Make the filling: put the ricotta, Parmesan, herbs, garlic and egg in a bowl, with salt and pepper to taste, and beat well to mix.

3 To make the sauce, put the walnuts, garlic and oil, with salt and pepper to taste, in a food processor and process to a paste, adding up to 125ml/4fl oz warm water to slacken the consistency. Spoon the mixture into a large bowl and add the cream. Beat well to mix, then adjust the seasoning if necessary.

4 Using a pasta machine, roll out one-quarter of the pasta to a 90–100cm/36–40in long strip. Cut the strip into two 45–50cm/18–20in lengths (you can do this during rolling if the strip becomes too long to manage).

5 Using a 5cm/2in square ravioli cutter, cut 8–10 squares from one of the pasta strips. Using a teaspoon, put a mound of filling in the centre of each square. Brush a

little water around the edge of each square, then fold the square diagonally in half over the filling to make a triangular shape, making sure there is little or no trapped air. Press gently to seal. Spread out the pansotti on a clean floured tea towel and sprinkle lightly with flour. Leave to dry while repeating the process with the remaining dough to make 64–80 pansotti altogether.

6 Put the pansotti in a large pan of boiling salted water, bring back to the boil, reduce the heat and poach at a gentle simmer for 4 –5 minutes.

7 Meanwhile, put the walnut sauce in a large warmed bowl and add a ladleful of the pasta cooking water to thin it down. Melt the butter in a small saucepan until sizzling. Drain the pansotti and tip them into the bowl of walnut sauce. Drizzle the butter over them. Toss well, then sprinkle with grated Parmesan.

8 Serve immediately, with more grated Parmesan handed around separately.

In Liguria, the dough for their version of ravioli, pansotti, is flavoured with white wine and fresh local herbs.

You can use Bolognese Sauce (page 164) instead of the besciamella.

Cannelloni with broad beans & ricotta

SERVES 6

FOR THE PASTA

150g/5oz Italian grade '00' flour
150g/5oz fine semolina, plus more for
  sprinkling
pinch of sea salt
2 large free-range eggs
1 tbsp olive oil

FOR THE FILLING

1kg/2¼lb broad beans in the pod, podded
350g/12oz ricotta
115g/4oz Pecorino Romano cheese, grated,
  plus more to serve

1 large garlic clove, crushed
large handful of mint, chopped
sea salt and freshly ground black pepper

FOR THE BESCIAMELLA SAUCE

600ml/1 pint milk
2 slices of onion
1 bay leaf
1 blade of mace
3 parsley stalks, bruised
5 whole black peppercorns
50g/2oz butter
45g/1½oz flour
150ml/¼ pint dry white wine

1 To make the pasta, heap the flour and semolina into a mound on the work surface. Sprinkle over the salt and mix well. Hollow out a well in the centre and break in the eggs. Add the olive oil and, with much care and patience, gradually work the eggs and oil into the flour until you have a slab of dough. Shape this into a ball and leave under a towel or in cling film to rest while you prepare the filling.

2 To make the filling, boil or steam the broad beans until tender, about 10 minutes. Drain and leave to cool. Once cool, put half of the beans in a food processor and pulse, leaving some texture. Add the ricotta, Pecorino, garlic and mint, with salt and pepper to taste. Add the remaining whole broad beans and mix well with a wooden spoon.

3 Roll out the pasta dough wafer thin and cut into 8cm/3in squares. Sprinkle lightly with semolina and let dry on a tray for 10–15 minutes.

4 When almost dry, cook the pasta squares in boiling salted water until al dente, i.e. just tender but still firm to the bite. Preheat the oven to 200°C/400°F/Gas 6.

5 To make the besciamella: place the milk in a pan with the onion slices, bay leaf, mace, parsley stalks and peppercorns. Heat over a medium-low heat and bring to a simmer, remove from the heat and leave to infuse for 8–10 minutes.

6 Melt 25g/1oz of butter in a saucepan, stir in the flour and continue stirring over the heat for 1 minute. Remove from the heat, strain in the infused milk and mix well. Return to the heat and stir or whisk continuously until boiling. Add the remaining butter and the wine and simmer for 3 minutes. Season to taste.

7 On each pasta square, spread a tablespoon of the broad bean filling and roll up into a cylinder. Spread half of the besciamella sauce in a casserole or baking dish, place in the filled cannelloni in parallel lines running from the long edge of the dish and cover with the remaining sauce. Sprinkle with the extra grated Pecorino cheese and bake in the oven for 15 minutes. Serve immediately.

These ravioli make good party nibbles, especially with a cold tomato sauce dip.

Fried ravioli

SERVES 6
FOR THE PASTA
300g/10½ oz strong white unbleached flour
   or plain white flour
pinch of sea salt
50g/2oz unsalted butter
1 egg, separated, plus 1 extra egg yolk
vegetable oil, for deep-frying

FOR THE FILLING
115g/4oz Gruyère cheese
85g/3oz fresh rocket, finely chopped
40g/1¼ oz freshly grated Parmesan cheese
1 egg, beaten
handful of flat-leaf parsley, finely chopped
sea salt and freshly ground black pepper

1 To make the pasta, sift the flour and salt on to a work surface. Make a well in the centre. Cut the butter into small dice and add with the egg yolks. Work to a smooth dough, adding a little lukewarm water if necessary.

2 To make the filling, grate the Gruyère cheese and put into a bowl with the rocket, Parmesan, beaten egg, parsley and salt and pepper to taste. Stir well together.

3 Flatten the pasta dough with a rolling pin and roll out into a sheet about 5mm/¼in thick. Cut into 12.5cm/5in rounds. Divide the filling between the rounds, placing it in the centre of each one. Lightly whisk the egg white. Brush the edges of the round with a little egg white, then fold the pasta over the filling to enclose it completely, ensuring that there is little or no trapped air, and pinch to seal.

4 Heat the oil for deep-frying to 190°C/375°F and drop in the ravioli, a few at a time, and cook until golden brown. Drain on absorbent kitchen paper, while frying the remaining ravioli. Serve hot.

Try frying the sage leaves until crisp before scattering them over the tortellini.

Tortellini with butter & sage

FOR THE PASTA

200g/7oz strong white unbleached flour, preferably Italian '00' grade, plus more for dusting

pinch of sea salt

2 large eggs

1 tbsp olive oil

FOR THE FILLING

100g/3½oz ricotta

50g/2oz Fontina cheese

50g/2oz freshly grated Parmesan cheese

1 egg, beaten

pinch of freshly grated nutmeg

handful of fresh sage leaves, finely chopped

TO FINISH

50g/2oz unsalted butter

handful of fresh sage leaves

freshly grated Parmesan cheese

1 Make the pasta dough as described on pages 10-13 and leave to rest in a cool place for about 30 minutes. Mix together all the filling ingredients and beat well.

2 Roll the dough out in a pasta machine as described on pages 14–17. Alternatively, divide the dough into manageable pieces and keep those you are not working on covered. Take one piece of dough and, with the heel of your hand, press it out. Using a long, thin rolling pin and a little flour, roll out the dough to a paper-thin sheet. Cut the pasta into 5cm/2in diameter circles. Place small spoonfuls of the filling on one side of each circle, dampen the edges, then fold the dough over the filling to make a half-moon (don't worry, the two edges won't quite meet), making sure there is little or no trapped air, and press down to seal. Curl the triangle around one of your index fingers, bringing the bottom two corners together, and press these together to seal. Leave to dry briefly on a flour-dusted tray.

3 Put the tortellini in a large saucepan of boiling salted water, adding a handful at a time, bring back to the boil, reduce the heat and poach at a gentle simmer for about 3–5 minutes. When they rise to the top of the pan, count 30 seconds, then remove with a slotted spoon and place in a warmed serving dish.

4 Melt the butter and pour over the tortellini. Garnish with sage leaves and serve with a sprinkling of Parmesan cheese.

Pork & turkey ravioli

SERVES 6–8

½ quantity egg pasta (see page 10–13)
flour, for dusting
50g/2oz butter
large bunch of fresh sage, leaves removed
  and roughly chopped, plus more to serve
4 tbsp freshly grated Parmesan cheese,
  plus more to serve

FOR THE FILLING
25g/1oz butter

150g/5oz minced pork
115g/4oz minced turkey
4 fresh sage leaves, finely chopped
sprig of rosemary, leaves removed and
  finely chopped
sea salt and freshly ground black pepper
2 tbsp dry white wine
65g/2¼oz ricotta cheese
3 tbsp grated Parmesan cheese
1 egg
freshly grated nutmeg

1 To make the filling: melt the butter in a pan, add the pork, turkey and the herbs. Cook for 5–6 minutes. Stir frequently and break up any lumps with a wooden spoon. Season with salt and pepper. Add the wine and stir again. Simmer for 1–2 minutes until reduced slightly. Cover the pan and simmer gently for about 20 minutes, stirring occasionally. With a slotted spoon, transfer the meat to a bowl and leave to cool.

2 Add the ricotta and Parmesan cheeses to the bowl of meat, together with the egg and freshly grated nutmeg to taste. Stir well to mix the ingredients thoroughly. Using a pasta machine, roll out one-quarter of the pasta dough into a 90–100cm/36–40in long strip. Cut the strip with a sharp knife into two 45–50cm/18–20in lengths (you can do this during rolling if the strips become too long to manage).

3 Use a teaspoon to make 10–12 evenly spaced little mounds of the filling along one side of one of the pasta strips. Brush a little water around each mound, then fold the plain side of the pasta strip over the filling. Starting from the folded edge, press down around each mound, pushing the air out at the unfolded edge. Sprinkle lightly with flour. With a fluted pasta wheel, cut along each long side in between the mounds to make small squares. Dust with flour. Put the ravioli on floured tea towels and leave to dry while repeating the process with the rest of the pasta to make 80–96 ravioli in total.

4 Drop the ravioli into a pan of salted boiling water, bring back to the boil, reduce the heat and simmer for 4–5 minutes. Meanwhile, melt the butter in a small pan. Remove the ravioli with a slotted spoon as they are cooked and serve dressed with the melted butter, herbs and cheese.

Pappardelle with rabbit sauce

SERVES 4

25g/1oz dried porcini mushrooms
175ml/6fl oz warm water
1 onion
1 carrot
1 celery stalk
3 bay leaves
25g/1oz unsalted butter
1 tbsp olive oil
50g/2oz pancetta
handful of flat-leaf parsley, roughly
    chopped, plus more to serve
250g/9oz boneless rabbit meat
6 tbsp dry white wine
200g/7oz can of chopped Italian plum
    tomatoes
sea salt and freshly ground black pepper
200g/7oz dried pappardelle

1 Put the dried mushrooms in a bowl, pour over the warm water and leave to reconstitute for 10–15 minutes. Finely chop the vegetables, either in a food processor or by hand. Make a tear in the bay leaves to help release their flavour.

2 Heat the butter and oil in a medium saucepan until just sizzling. Add the chopped vegetables, pancetta and parsley, and cook for 5 minutes.

3 Add the rabbit meat and fry on all sides for 3–4 minutes. Pour the wine over and let it reduce for a few minutes, then add the tomatoes. Drain the mushrooms and pour the soaking liquid into the pan. Chop the mushrooms and add them to the mixture with the bay leaves and salt and pepper to taste. Stir well, cover and simmer for 35–45 minutes until the rabbit is tender, stirring occasionally.

4 Remove the pan from the heat and lift out the rabbit pieces with a slotted spoon. Cut them into bite-sized chunks and stir them back into the sauce. Remove and discard the bay leaves. Taste and adjust the seasoning if necessary.

5 Cook the pasta in boiling salted water until al dente, i.e. just tender but still firm to the bite.

6 Reheat the sauce if necessary. Drain the pasta and toss with the sauce in a warmed bowl. Serve immediately, sprinkled with parsley.

This sauce is one that definitely improves in flavour for being made at least a day ahead and then reheated.

Spaghetti with veal meatballs

SERVES 6–8

350g/12oz dried spaghetti

freshly grated Parmesan cheese, to serve

FOR THE MEATBALL SAUCE

350g/12oz minced veal

1 egg

2 tbsp roughly chopped flat-leaf parsley,
   plus more to serve

sea salt and freshly ground black pepper

1 thick slice of white bread, crusts removed

2 tbsp milk

3 tbsp olive oil

300ml/½ pint passata

400ml/14fl oz vegetable stock

1 tsp sugar

1 Make the meatballs: put the veal in a large bowl, add the egg and half of the parsley. Season with salt and pepper. Tear the bread into small pieces and place in a small bowl. Moisten with the milk and leave to soak for a few minutes. Squeeze out the excess milk and crumble the bread over the meat mixture. Mix everything together with a wooden spoon, then use your hands to squeeze and knead the mixture so that it becomes smooth and sticky.

2 Wash your hands, rinse them under cold running water, then pick up small pieces of the mixture and roll them between the palms of your hands to make about 40–60 small balls. Place the meatballs on a tray and chill for 30 minutes.

3 Heat the oil in a large frying pan and cook the meatballs in batches until browned.

4 Pour the passata and stock into a large saucepan, heat gently, then add the sugar, with salt and pepper to taste. Add the meatballs, then bring to the boil. Lower the heat, cover and simmer for 20 minutes.

5 Cook the pasta in boiling salted water until al dente, i.e. just tender but still firm to the bite.

6 Drain the pasta and tip it into a warmed large bowl. Pour the sauce over the pasta and toss gently. Sprinkle with the remaining parsley and serve with Parmesan cheese.

Lasagne with meatballs

SERVES 6-8
275g/11oz minced beef
275g/11oz minced pork
1 large egg
50g/2oz fresh white breadcrumbs
5 tbsp freshly grated Parmesan cheese
2 tbsp chopped fresh flat-leaf parsley
2 garlic cloves, crushed
sea salt and freshly ground black pepper
4 tbsp olive oil
1 onion, finely chopped
1 carrot, finely chopped
1 celery stalk, finely chopped

2 x 400g/14oz cans of chopped Italian plum
 tomatoes
2 tsp finely chopped fresh oregano or basil
6-8 no-need-to-precook dried lasagne
 sheets

FOR THE BESCIAMELLA SAUCE
700ml/1¼ pints milk
1 bay leaf
1 fresh thyme sprig
50g/2oz unsalted butter
50g/2oz Italian grade '00' flour or plain flour
freshly grated nutmeg

1 Make the meatballs: put 175g/6oz each of the minced beef and pork in a bowl.
Add the egg, breadcrumbs, 2 tablespoons of the Parmesan, half the parsley, half the
garlic and plenty of salt and pepper. Mix everything together with a wooden spoon.
Use your hands to squeeze and knead the mixture until it is smooth and quite sticky.

2 Wash your hands, rinse them under cold running water, then pick up small pieces
of the mixture and roll between your palms to make about 30 walnut-sized balls.
Place on a tray and chill for about 30 minutes.

3 Meanwhile, put the milk for the besciamella sauce in a saucepan. Make a tear in
the bay leaf, then add it and the thyme sprig to the milk and bring to the boil. Remove
from the heat, cover and leave to infuse.

4 Make the meat sauce: heat half the oil in a pan, add the onion, carrot, celery and
remaining garlic. Stir over a low heat for 5 minutes, until softened. Add the remaining
minced meats and cook gently for 10 minutes, stirring frequently. Break up any lumps.
Stir in salt and pepper to taste, then add the tomatoes, remaining parsley and the
oregano or basil. Stir well, cover and simmer for 45-60 minutes, stirring occasionally.

5 Meanwhile, heat the remaining oil in a large non-stick frying pan. When hot, cook the meatballs in batches over a medium-to-high heat for 5–8 minutes until browned all over. Shake the pan from time to time so that the meatballs roll around. As they cook, transfer them to kitchen paper to drain.

6 Preheat the oven to 190°C/375°F/Gas 5. Make the besciamella sauce: strain the milk to remove the bay and thyme. Melt the butter in a medium pan, add the flour and cook, stirring, for 1–2 minutes. Add the milk, a little at a time, whisking vigorously after each addition. Bring to the boil and cook, stirring constantly, until thick and smooth. Grate in a little nutmeg to taste and season with salt and pepper. Whisk well, then remove from the heat.

7 Spread one-third of the meat sauce in the bottom of a large shallow baking dish. Add half of the meatballs, spread with one-third of the besciamella and cover with half the lasagne sheets. Repeat these layers, then top with the remaining meat sauce and besciamella. Sprinkle the remaining grated Parmesan evenly over the surface.

8 Bake for 30–40 minutes or until golden brown and bubbling. Allow to stand for 10 minutes before serving. If you like, garnish each serving with parsley.

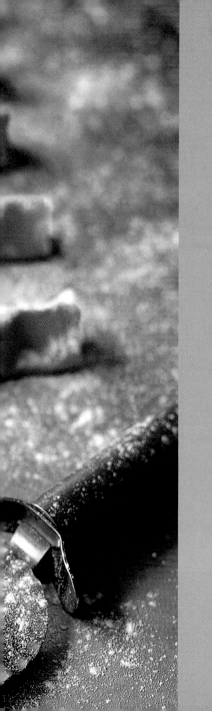

pasta to impress

Pasta has become so much a part of everyday family eating in this country that people often look askance at me when I suggest serving it at dinner parties or for special occasions. Nevertheless, pasta can be rich and luxurious, and every bit as impressive as a roast or an elaborate layered chef's extravaganza. Certain ingredients immediately endow pasta with that touch of class – crab and lobster in fillings for stuffed pasta, say, or saffron to colour the pasta. Some techniques do it, like open layered lasagne (**Vincisgrassi Aperto**) or stuffed rolls of pasta, sliced and grilled (**Rotolo Ripieno**). Essentially, however, the dishes remain simple, and it is the shape of the pasta and dramatic or unusual presentation that do the job.

Cheese cappellacci with bolognese sauce

SERVES 6–8

½ quantity of fresh egg pasta (page 10–13)
flour, for dusting
2 litres/3½ pt beef stock (page 42)
freshly grated Parmesan cheese, to serve
basil leaves, to garnish

FOR THE FILLING

250g/9oz ricotta cheese
85g/3oz Taleggio cheese, rind removed and
diced very small
4 tbsp freshly grated Parmesan cheese
1 small egg
freshly grated nutmeg
sea salt and freshly ground black pepper

FOR THE BOLOGNESE SAUCE

25g/1oz butter
1 tbsp olive oil
1 onion, finely chopped
2 carrots, finely chopped
2 celery stalks, finely chopped
2 garlic cloves, finely chopped
115g/4oz pancetta, cut into small cubes
250g/9oz lean minced pork
250g/9oz lean minced beef
125ml/4fl oz dry white wine
2 x 400g/14oz cans of chopped Italian plum
tomatoes
450–750ml/16–26fl oz beef stock
100ml/3½fl oz double cream

1 To make the filling: put the ricotta, Taleggio and grated Parmesan cheese in a bowl and mash together with a fork. Add the egg and freshly grated nutmeg with salt and pepper to taste, and stir well to mix.

2 Using a pasta machine, roll out one-quarter of the pasta into a 90 x 100cm/ 36 x 40in strip. Cut the strip with a sharp knife into 45–50cm/18–20in lengths. Using a 6–7.5cm/2½–3in square ravioli cutter, cut 6 or 7 squares from one of the pasta strips. Using a teaspoon, put a mound of filling in the centre of each square. Brush a little water around the edge of each square, then fold the square diagonally in half over the filling to make a triangular shape. Press to seal. Wrap the triangle around one of your index fingers, bringing the bottom two corners together. Pinch the ends together to seal, then press with your fingertips around the top edge of the filling to make an indentation so that the 'hat' looks like a bishop's mitre. Put the cappellacci on floured clean tea towels, sprinkle with flour and leave to dry while repeating the process with the remaining dough to make 48–56 cappellacci in total.

3 To make the Bolognese Sauce: heat the butter and oil in a large saucepan until sizzling. Add the vegetables, garlic and pancetta, and cook over a medium heat, stirring frequently, for 10 minutes or until the vegetables have softened. Add the meats, lower the heat and cook gently for 10 minutes, stirring frequently and breaking up any lumps in the meat with a wooden spoon. Stir in salt and pepper to taste, then add the wine and stir again. Simmer for about 5 minutes or until reduced.

4 Add the tomatoes and 250ml/9fl oz of the stock, and bring to the boil. Stir well then lower the heat, half cover the pan with a lid and leave to simmer very gently for 2 hours. Stir occasionally and add more stock as it becomes absorbed.

5 Add the cream to the meat sauce. Stir well to mix, then simmer the sauce for another 30 minutes, stirring frequently.

6 Bring the stock for cooking the pasta to the boil in a large saucepan, drop the cappellacci into it, bring back to the boil, reduce the heat and poach at a gentle simmer for 4–5 minutes. Drain the cappellacci and divide them among 6–8 warmed bowls. Spoon the hot Bolognese Sauce over the cappellacci and sprinkle with grated Parmesan and basil leaves. Serve immediately.

Spinach, ricotta & tomato pasta roll

SERVES 4
½ quantity of egg pasta (see page 10–13)
25g/1oz unsalted butter, melted, plus more
   for greasing
50g/2oz freshly grated Parmesan cheese

FOR THE FILLING
4 plum tomatoes
350g/12oz fresh spinach
175g/6oz ricotta
freshly grated nutmeg
sea salt and freshly grated black pepper
50g/2oz freshly grated Parmesan cheese

1 Start by preparing the filling: put the tomatoes in a small bowl and cover with boiling water for about 40 seconds, then plunge them into cold water. Skin and chop the flesh.

2 Put the spinach in a saucepan with only the water still clinging to the leaves after washing. Cook for about 5 minutes over a medium-high heat. Drain the spinach well, squeezing out as much excess water as you can.

3 Finely chop the drained spinach and put it in a medium-sized bowl. Add the tomatoes and ricotta, with nutmeg, salt and pepper to taste. Mix everything together with the Parmesan cheese.

4 Roll the pasta dough out to a rectangular sheet about 3mm/⅛in thick. Place it on a large piece of muslin and spread the filling over the dough, leaving a 3cm/1¼in border clear around the edge. By lifting one end of the muslin, roll up the dough like a Swiss roll. Wrap it in the muslin and secure the ends with string so it looks a bit like a Christmas cracker.

5 Place the roll in a long, narrow flameproof casserole, roasting tin or fish kettle and cover with lightly salted cold water. Bring to the boil and simmer for 30 minutes. Remove from the water and leave to cool for about 5 minutes. Preheat the grill to a very hot setting.

6 Remove the muslin and cut the roll into slices about 2cm/¾ in thick. Place these side by side, or slightly overlapping, in a buttered heatproof dish. Pour the melted butter over the slices, sprinkle them with the Parmesan and grill for 5 minutes until golden. Serve immediately, straight from the dish or on serving plates, sprinkled with a little black pepper and more melted butter or extra-virgin olive oil.

The pasta roll can be made in advance and kept, wrapped, in the fridge for up to 2 days. First, allow it to return to room temperature, then slice and grill as above.

Any pasta that you have leftover can be used just like pastry, to line, say, a pie or quiche dish.

Garganelli with asparagus & cream

SERVES 4

bunch of fresh young asparagus (about
250–350g/9–12oz)

sea salt and freshly ground black pepper

350g/12oz dried garganelli

25g/1oz unsalted butter

200ml/7fl oz double cream

2 tbsp dry white wine

85–115g/3–4oz freshly grated Parmesan
cheese

2 tbsp chopped mixed fresh herbs (basil,
flat-leaf parsley, marjoram and oregano)

1 Trim off and throw away the woody end of the asparagus (after trimming you should have about 200g/7oz of asparagus spears). Cut the spears at an angle into pieces that are roughly the same length and shape as the garganelli.

2 Reserving the tips, blanch the asparagus spears in boiling salted water for 2 minutes, adding the tips for the second minute only. Immediately drain the asparagus spears and tips, rinse in cold water and set aside.

3 Cook the pasta in boiling salted water until al dente, i.e. just tender but still firm to the bite.

4 Meanwhile, put the butter and cream in a medium saucepan, add salt and pepper to taste and bring to the boil. Simmer for a few minutes until the cream reduces slightly and thickens. Add the asparagus, wine and about half the grated Parmesan. Taste and adjust the seasoning if necessary. Keep on a low heat.

5 Drain the cooked pasta and tip it into a warm bowl. Pour over the sauce, sprinkle with herbs and toss well. Serve topped with the remaining Parmesan.

Garganelli are made from little squares of pasta rolled into quill shapes and then grooved. You could use penne instead.

Cannelloni with saffron sauce

SERVES 2

4 sheets of lasagne, each about
   16 x 12.5cm/6½ x 5in
sea salt and freshly ground black pepper

FOR THE FILLING

2 tbsp olive oil
1 small onion, chopped
4 canned artichoke hearts, drained,
   rinsed and chopped
50g/2oz mozzarella cheese, chopped

115g/4oz ricotta cheese
50g/2oz Dolcelatte cheese
1 tsp finely chopped fresh rosemary

FOR THE SAUCE

15g/½oz unsalted butter
½ garlic clove, crushed
large pinch of saffron strands
1 tbsp white wine
125g/4oz mascarpone cheese
sea salt and freshly ground black pepper

1 Preheat the oven to 180°C/350°F/Gas 4. Put the pasta in a large saucepan of boiling salted water and bring back to the boil. Boil for 1–2 minutes, then drain and rinse under cold water.

2 To make the filling, heat the oil in a saucepan, add the onion and fry until soft. Add the chopped artichokes and cook for 5 minutes. Add the mozzarella, ricotta, Dolcelatte cheese and rosemary. Season well with salt and pepper and mix well together.

3 To make the sauce, melt the butter in a saucepan, add the garlic and saffron and heat gently. Add the wine and mascarpone cheese, with salt and pepper to taste, and simmer for 5 minutes.

4 To assemble the dish, place some filling down the centre of each pasta sheet. Moisten the edges with water and roll each rectangle up from one of its narrow edges to form a thick tube. Arrange the cannelloni in a greased ovenproof dish, pour the sauce over and cover with foil.

5 Bake in the oven for 20 minutes, then serve immediately.

Bonbons with wild mushrooms & Ricotta

**SERVES 6 AS A STARTER OR
4 AS A MAIN COURSE**
6 sheets of fresh egg pasta (see note
 below), about 28 x 24cm/11 x 9½in
1 egg, lightly beaten

FOR THE FILLING
200g/7oz wild mushrooms, finely chopped
150g/5oz flat mushrooms, finely chopped
½ onion, grated
150g/5oz ricotta cheese

2 tbsp freshly grated Parmesan cheese
½ tsp finely chopped fresh sage
½ tsp finely chopped fresh oregano
½ tsp finely chopped fresh parsley
pinch of freshly grated nutmeg
freshly ground black pepper

TO FINISH
single cream or melted butter, for coating
freshly grated Parmesan cheese

1 Cut each pasta sheet into 9 rectangles, each about 7.5 x 5cm/3 x 2in. Using a scalloped pastry wheel, trim the shorter ends of each rectangle.

2 Mix all the filling ingredients together. Place a teaspoon of filling in the centre of each pasta rectangle. Brush the beaten egg down one long side and fold the pasta to form a tube. Press to seal, trying to remove as much trapped air as possible, then pinch and twist the ends tightly, like a bonbon wrapper. As each bonbon is made, set it aside, uncovered, to rest.

3 Drop the bonbons, a few at a time, into a large saucepan of boiling salted water, bring back to the boil, reduce the heat and then poach at a gentle simmer for 4–5 minutes or until just tender. Remove with a slotted spoon and pile into a warmed serving dish.

4 Toss in cream or butter and sprinkle with Parmesan cheese to serve.

These are best made with thinly rolled pasta. Use the recipe on page 11 but use only 200g/7oz of each flour and 4 eggs.

The bonbons also suit a herb or spinach and ricotta stuffing (see pages 140 and 169).

Tagliatelle with radicchio & cream

SERVES 4
225g/8oz dried tagliatelle
sea salt and freshly ground black pepper
85g/3oz pancetta or bacon, diced
25g/1oz unsalted butter
1 onion, finely chopped

115–175g/4–6oz radicchio, shredded
1 garlic clove, finely chopped
150ml/¼ pint double cream
50g/2oz grated Parmesan cheese
handful of flat-leaf parsley, chopped

1 Cook the pasta in boiling salted water until al dente, i.e. just tender but still firm to the bite.

2 Meanwhile, gently heat the pancetta or bacon in a pan until the fat runs. Increase the heat and stir-fry for 5 minutes. Add the butter, onion and radicchio, and stir-fry for 4 minutes. Add the garlic and stir-fry for 1 minute more, until the onion is lightly coloured. Pour in the cream and add the Parmesan with seasoning to taste. Stir-fry for 1–2 minutes until bubbling. Adjust the seasoning.

3 Drain the pasta, tip into a bowl, pour over the sauce and toss well with the parsley.

Garganelli with salmon & prawns

SERVES 4

350g/12oz salmon fillets
200ml/7fl oz dry white wine
a few basil leaves, plus more to garnish
sea salt and freshly ground black pepper

150ml/¼ pint double cream
6 ripe plum tomatoes, skinned and finely
 chopped
350g/12oz garganelli
115g/4oz peeled cooked prawns

1 Put the salmon in a wide shallow pan, skin-side up. Pour over the wine, scatter in the basil and sprinkle with salt and pepper. Bring to the boil, cover and simmer gently for no more than 5 minutes. Use a fish slice to lift the fish out. Set aside to cool slightly.

2 Add the cream and tomatoes to the liquid remaining in the pan and bring to the boil. Stir well, lower the heat and simmer, uncovered, for 10–15 minutes until it thickens slightly.

3 Meanwhile, cook the pasta in a large saucepan of boiling salted water until al dente, i.e. just tender but still firm to the bite.

4 When cool enough to handle, flake the fish into large chunks, carefully discarding the skin and any bones. Add the fish to the sauce, together with the prawns, shaking the pan until the fish and shellfish are well coated. Taste and adjust the seasoning.

5 Drain the cooked pasta and tip it into a warmed serving bowl. Spoon the sauce over the pasta and toss well to combine. Serve immediately, garnished with more basil leaves.

Garganelli are made from little squares of pasta rolled into quill shapes and then grooved. You could use penne instead.

Ravioli with crab

SERVES 4

½ quantity of fresh egg pasta (page 11)
flour, for dusting
90g/3¼oz unsalted butter
juice of 1 lemon

FOR THE FILLING

175g/6oz mascarpone cheese
175g/6oz crab meat
handful of finely chopped fresh flat-leaf
  parsley
finely grated zest of 1 unwaxed lemon
sea salt and freshly ground black pepper

1 First make the filling: put the mascarpone in a bowl, mash well with a fork and add the crab meat, parsley and lemon zest with salt and pepper to taste. Stir well.

2 Using a pasta machine, roll out one-quarter of the pasta into a 90–100cm/36–40in strip. With a sharp knife, cut the strip into four 45–50cm/18–20in lengths (you can do this during the rolling if the strip gets too long to manage). Using a 6cm/2½in fluted biscuit cutter, cut out 8 discs from each pasta strip.

3 Using a teaspoon, put a mound of filling in the centre of half the discs. Brush a little water around the edge of the filled discs, then top each with another disc and press the edges to seal, trying to eliminate as much trapped air as you can. For a decorative finish, press the edges with the tines of a fork.

4 Put the ravioli on a floured dish, sprinkle lightly with flour and leave to dry while repeating the process with the remaining dough and filling to make 32 ravioli in all. Add the ravioli to a large saucepan of boiling salted water, bring back to the boil, reduce the heat and then poach at a gentle simmer for 4–5 minutes.

5 Meanwhile, melt the butter with the lemon juice until sizzling. Drain the ravioli and divide them equally among 4 warmed bowls. Drizzle the lemon butter over the ravioli and serve immediately.

You could use all white crab meat or a mixture of white and dark. Dark meat will give a much stronger flavour.

Buy fresh scallops with their coral if possible. They always have a better texture and flavour than frozen scallops.

Tagliatelle with scallops & chilli

SERVES 4

200g/7oz scallops, each sliced across into
  2 discs
2 tbsp plain flour
sea salt and freshly ground black pepper
45g/1½oz unsalted butter
1 small onion, finely chopped

1 small fresh red chilli, deseeded and
  very finely chopped
2 tbsp finely chopped fresh
  flat-leaf parsley
4 tbsp brandy
7 tbsp fish stock
350g/12oz tagliatelle

1 Toss the scallops in the flour, then shake off the excess. Bring a saucepan of salted water to the boil ready for cooking the pasta.

2 Meanwhile, melt the butter in a saucepan. Add the onion, chilli and half the parsley, and fry over a medium heat, stirring frequently, for 1–2 minutes. Add the scallops and toss over the heat for 1–2 minutes.

3 Pour the brandy over the scallops and immediately (and carefully) set it alight with a match. As soon as the flames have died down, stir in the fish stock, with salt and pepper to taste. Mix well, simmer for 2–3 minutes, then cover the pan and remove it from the heat.

4 Add the pasta to the boiling water and cook it until al dente, i.e. just tender but still firm to the bite.

5 Drain the pasta, add to the sauce and toss over a medium heat until mixed. Serve at once, sprinkling over the remaining parsley.

Strangozzi, chicken & courgette flowers

SERVES 4

sea salt and freshly ground black pepper
2 skinless chicken breasts, 350g/12oz total
50g/2oz unsalted butter
2 tbsp olive oil
1 small onion, thinly sliced
200g/7oz small courgettes, cut into thin
  julienne strips

1 garlic clove, crushed
2 tsp finely chopped fresh marjoram
350g/12oz dried strangozzi
large handful of courgette flowers,
  thoroughly washed and dried
thinly shaved Parmesan cheese, to garnish

1 Season the chicken and grill under a medium heat, turning once, for 25 minutes until golden. Cut into evenly sized pieces and put to one side.

2 Heat the butter and half the olive oil in a medium saucepan, add the onion and cook gently, stirring frequently, for about 5 minutes until softened. Add the courgettes to the pan and sprinkle over the garlic, marjoram and salt and pepper to taste. Add the chicken pieces and cook for 8 minutes until the courgettes have coloured.

3 Meanwhile, cook the pasta in a large saucepan of boiling salted water until al dente, i.e. just tender but still firm to the bite.

4 Set aside a few whole courgette flowers for garnish, then roughly shred the rest and add them to the courgette mixture. Stir to mix, taste and adjust the seasoning.

5 Drain the cooked pasta, tip it into a warmed large bowl and add the remaining oil. Toss, add the courgette mixture and toss again. Top with Parmesan shavings and the reserved courgette flowers.

Strangozzi are a small version of strozzapreti or 'priest stranglers', a short, twisted pasta from Modena. You could use spaghetti instead.

Open lasagne with ceps & Parma ham

SERVES 4–6
½ quantity fresh egg pasta (page 10–13)
sea salt and freshly ground black pepper
400g/14oz fresh porcini mushrooms, sliced
4 tbsp extra-virgin olive oil
200g/7oz Parma ham, cut into
  julienne strips
200ml/7fl oz single cream
3 tbsp freshly chopped parsley

150g/5oz freshly grated Parmesan cheese
white truffle oil or, if possible, a little
  shaved white truffle

FOR THE SAUCE
150g/5oz unsalted butter
50g/2oz plain flour, preferably grade '00'
  Italian flour
1.2 litres/2 pints milk, heated

1 Roll the dough through the pasta machine as you would for lasagne. Cut the pasta lengths into 12.5cm/5in squares. Cook the squares, a few at a time, in plenty of boiling salted water. Place on clean kitchen towels to drain.

2 Make the sauce: melt 50g/2oz of the butter, add the flour and blend in well. Add the hot milk, a little at a time, beating well with a batter whisk.

3 Cook the porcini in the olive oil until softened and add to the sauce. Stir in the Parma ham, cream and parsley. Season and bring to the boil. Remove from the heat.

4 Preheat the oven to 220°C/425°F/Gas 7. To assemble the vincisgrassi, butter a gratin dish (or individual gratin dishes) and cover the butter with a layer of pasta. Then spread over a layer of besciamella, dot with butter and sprinkle with some Parmesan cheese. Continue the process, making layer after layer, finishing with a besciamella layer and sprinkling of Parmesan cheese. Bake for 20 minutes until bubbling. Finish under a hot grill, if necessary, to give the top a good colour.

5 Serve with a little splash or two of truffle oil or, best of all, shavings of white truffle, and a little more Parmesan cheese.

Neapolitan ricotta tart

SERVES 10

FOR THE PASTRY

225g/8oz unsalted butter

175g/6oz caster sugar

4 egg yolks

450g/1lb plain or Italian grade '00' flour,
plus more for dusting

FOR THE FILLING

450g/1lb ricotta cheese

115g/4oz caster sugar

1 tsp ground cinnamon

grated zest and juice of 1 unwaxed lemon

4 tbsp orange flower water

115g/4oz candied orange or mixed peel

1 free-range egg, separated

550ml/scant 1 pint milk

175g/6oz vermicelli

large pinch of salt

icing sugar, for dusting

1 To make the pastry: put the butter and sugar in a bowl and cream together. Add the egg yolks and then gradually add the flour, mixing well to make a soft dough. Wrap in greaseproof paper and chill in the fridge for 30 minutes.

2 To make the filling, put the ricotta, sugar (reserving 2 tablespoons), cinnamon, half the lemon zest, the lemon juice, the orange flower water, candied peel and the egg yolk in a bowl, and beat together.

3 In a small saucepan, bring the milk to the boil. Add the vermicelli and the remaining sugar and lemon zest with the salt and simmer gently until the vermicelli has absorbed nearly all the milk.

4 While it is still warm, blend the pasta carefully into the ricotta mixture. Whisk the egg white until it just holds its shape, then fold into the mixture.

5 Preheat the oven to 190°C/375°F/Gas 5. On a lightly floured surface, roll out the pastry and use two-thirds of it to line a 28cm/11in loose-bottomed flan tin. It is a very short pastry, so it may tear readily but you can patch it very easily.

6 Add the ricotta filling, then cut the remaining pastry into 5mm/¼in strips and arrange in a lattice pattern over the top of the tart.

7 Bake in the oven for 40–50 minutes until golden. Dust with icing sugar before serving warm or cold.

Acknowledgements

The publishers wish to thank the following for the loan of props for photography:

The Conran Shop, www.conran.com; **Divertimenti**, www.divertimenti.co.uk; **Designers Guild**, www.designersguild.com; **Habitat**, www.habitat.net; **Ikea**, www.ikea.com; **Inventory**; **Jerry's**; **LSA International**, www.lsa-international.com; **Muji**, www.mujionline.co.uk.

Food Stylists Maxine Clark, Joanna Farrow, Marie Ange Lapierre, Louise Pickford, Bridget Sargeson, Linda Tubby

Photographic Stylists Kasha Harmer Hirst, Maya Babic

Contributors Sara Buenfeld, Maxine Clark, Joanna Farrow, Janet Illsley, Louise Pickford, Bridget Sargeson, Linda Tubby, Sunil Vijayakar